An Analysis of

Jean Lave and Etienne Wenger's

Situated Learning: Legitimate Peripheral Participation

T0383102

Charmi Patel

Published by Macat International Ltd
24:13 Coda Centre, 189 Munster Road, London SW6 6AW.

Distributed exclusively by Routledge
2 Park Square, Milton Park, Abingdon, Oxon OX14 4RN
711 Third Avenue, New York, NY 10017, USA

Routledge is an imprint of the Taylor & Francis Group, an informa business

www.macat.com
info@macat.com

Cataloguing in Publication Data
A catalogue record for this book is available from the British Library.
Library of Congress Cataloguing-in-Publication Data is available upon request.
Cover illustration: A. Richard Allen

ISBN 978-1-912302-15-4 (hardback)
ISBN 978-1-912128-61-7 (paperback)
ISBN 978-1-912281-03-9 (e-book)

'Macat is taking on some of the major challenges in university education ... They have drawn together a strong team of active academics who are producing teaching materials that are novel in the breadth of their approach.'

'The Macat vision is exceptionally exciting. It focuses upon new modes of learning which analyse and explain seminal texts which have profoundly influenced world thinking and so social and economic development. It promotes the kind of critical thinking which is essential for any society and economy. This is the learning of the future.'

'The Macat analyses provide immediate access to the critical conversation surrounding the books that have shaped their respective discipline, which will make them an invaluable resource to all of those, students and teachers, working in the field.'

'Listening to classical music or jazz without having had a musical training, you can like the piece, but you don't know why or even what the musician/composer is doing in it, let alone its significance in the history of music as a whole. Similarly there is so much implicit in an academic text that to read it out of the context in which it is written requires some pointers to help you understand the author, their concerns, and what they were responding to; in short, the intellectual history of the work. This is where Macat comes in, not as a substitute but as an essential complement to the writing of seminal figures in the history of a discipline.'

ABOUT THE AUTHOR OF THE ORIGINAL WORK

Born in 1939 in the United States, **Jean Lave** is an anthropologist and professor at the University of California, Berkeley. Most of her career has been focused on social aspects of the learning process, and she continues to write and teach.

Her collaborator **Etienne Wenger** was born in Switzerland in 1952. He holds a doctorate in artificial intelligence, and teamed up with Lave when both were at the Institute for Research on Learning in Palo Alto, California. Wenger is now an independent consultant helping organizations establish "communities of practice," a term the pair coined for groups organized around a common interest, and in which individuals learn from each other through active participation.

ABOUT THE AUTHORS OF THE ANALYSIS

Dr Charmi Patel is an associate professor at the Henley Business School at the University of Reading. She holds a PhD in Organisational Behaviour and an MSc in Human Resource Management from the Aston Business School, Aston University, and has taught at the University of Edinburgh Business School. There she was also the Programme Director, for Edinburgh's MSc in International Human Resource management, having designed and launched the MSc programme from its inception until 2016. Her research uses the concepts of resource management and organizational behavior to examine the ways in which individuals relate to their work and to the organizations that employ them.

ABOUT THIS BOOK

This book is part of a series of unique academic explorations of seminal works in the humanities and social sciences – books and papers that have had a significant and widely recognised impact on their disciplines. It has been created to serve as much more than just a summary of what lies between the covers of a great book. It illuminates and explores the influences on, ideas of, and impact of that book. Our goal is to offer a learning resource that encourages critical thinking and fosters a better, deeper understanding of important ideas.

Each publication is divided into three parts, which we call Sections. They are: Influences, Ideas, and Impact.

Each Section has four chapters, which we call Modules. These explore every important facet of the work, and the responses to it. You can find a list in the Contents.

This Section-Module structure makes a Macat book easy to use, but it has another important feature. Because each Macat book is written to the same format, it is possible (and encouraged!) to cross-reference multiple Macat books along the same lines of inquiry or research. This allows the reader to open up interesting interdisciplinary pathways.

To further aid your reading, lists of glossary terms and people mentioned are included at the end of this book (these are indicated by an asterisk [*] throughout) – as well as a list of works cited.

We've partnered with some of the best academic minds in the world to produce these publications.

We hope you enjoy your Macat journey. Read this book critically and let us know what you think at **www.macat.com.**

CRITICAL THINKING AND *SITUATED LEARNING*

Primary critical thinking skill: CREATIVE THINKING
Secondary critical thinking skill: ANALYSIS

Social anthropologist Jean Lave and computer scientist Etienne Wenger's seminal *Situated Learning* helped change the fields of cognitive science and pedagogy by approaching learning from a novel angle. Traditionally, theories of learning and education had focused on processes of cognition – the mental processes of knowledge formation that occur within an individual. Lave and Wenger chose to look at learning not as an individual process, but a social one.

As so often with the creative thinking process, a small, simple shift in emphasis was all that was required to show things in an entirely different light. What *Situated Learning* illustrated – and emphasized – was that learning is dependent on its social situation. Even though the most effective way to learn is through interaction with experts and peers in a community organized around a common interest, the traditional cognitive learning model failed to account for the way in which learners interact with their 'community of practice.' The new hypothesis that Lave and Wenger developed was that learning can be seen as a continuously evolving set of relationships situated within a social context. This allowed Lave and Wenger to place discussions of apprenticeship and workplace learning on a new footing – and led in turn to the book's impressive impact in business and management scholarship.

Macat has worked with the University of Cambridge to identify the elements of critical thinking and understand the ways in which six different skills combine to enable effective thinking. Three allow us to fully understand a problem; three more give us the tools to solve it. Together, these six skills make up the **PACIER** model of critical thinking. They are:

ANALYSIS – understanding how an argument is built
EVALUATION – exploring the strengths and weaknesses of an argument
INTERPRETATION – understanding issues of meaning

CREATIVE THINKING – coming up with new ideas and fresh connections
PROBLEM-SOLVING – producing strong solutions
REASONING – creating strong arguments

To find out more, visit **WWW.MACAT.COM.**

CONTENTS

WAYS IN TO THE TEXT

KEY POINTS

- The social anthropologist* Jean Lave and the computer scientist Etienne Wenger coauthored *Situated Learning* (1991) while at the Californian not-for-profit Institute for Research on Learning* (social anthropology is a discipline looking at the ways in which our social institutions and behavior reflect the defining characteristics of our species).

- By focusing on the social aspects of learning, the book gives a new dimension to the concept of apprenticeship* (on-the-job training).

- *Situated Learning* considers theories of meaning, practice, learning, and identity* (the characteristics understood to determine who we are); it is relevant to the fields of psychology* (the study of the human mind and behavior), linguistics* (the study of the nature and functioning of language), anthropology* (the study of human culture, belief, and practices), and educational science.

Who Are Jean Lave and Etienne Wenger?

Born in the United States in 1939, Jean Lave, the coauthor of *Situated Learning: Legitimate Peripheral Participation*, is a social anthropologist based at the University of California, Berkeley, with an interest in social theory. Much of her research concentrates on learning, learners, and everyday life as it is understood in the context of society. In addition to *Situated Learning*, Lave has written three books with this focus: *Everyday Cognition: Its Development in Social Context* (coedited with Barbara Rogoff, 1984), *Cognition in Practice* (1988), and *Understanding Practice* (coauthored with the social scientist Seth Chaiklin, 1993).[1]

Born in Switzerland in 1952, Etienne Wenger received his bachelor's degree in computer science from the University of Geneva, his master's in information and computer science in 1984, and a doctorate in artificial intelligence in 1990, both from the University of California, Irvine. He then joined the Institute for Research on Learning in Palo Alto, California, an institute dedicated to research in the field of learning. He considers himself a social learning* theorist (one who studies theories of how knowledge is transmitted through social processes) as his work focuses on learning that takes place at the social or group level, and not just within an individual mind. Wenger is now an independent consultant specializing in helping organizations develop "communities of practice"*—a term coined by the authors to describe a group of people ("practitioners") organized around a similar interest, with access to a similar body of knowledge on the topic.

In addition to *Situated Learning*, Wenger has written and coauthored several books in the field of social learning, including *Communities of Practice: Learning, Meaning, and Identity* (1998), in which he lays out a theory of learning; *Cultivating Communities of Practice: A Guide to Managing Knowledge* (2002), coauthored with the social scientists Richard McDermott and William M. Snyder and addressed to those who want to develop communities of practice in their own organizations; and *Digital Habitats* (2009), with Nancy White and John D. Smith, which focuses on issues related to the use of technology. Wenger's contributions extend beyond education studies to address the importance of the concept of communities of practice in public and private organizations in areas including business, government, international development, healthcare, and education.

According to Infed, the education community website, Lave and Wenger's *Situated Learning* provided "path-breaking analysis" and "set the scene for some significant innovations in practice within organizations, and more recently within some schools."[2]

What Does *Situated Learning* Say?

Situated Learning is a pioneering book on social theories of learning. In contrast to previous schools of thought in education studies that focused on cognition*—the processing of information to form knowledge in the mind of the individual[3]—the work emphasizes learning in the context of a social situation.

By proposing a social account of learning, *Situated Learning* contributes to the intellectual debates of its time by questioning the significance of individual psychology throughout the learning process. It does so by arguing that learning is largely the function of its social context, which is affected by historical and political forces. As such, learning is *situated* because it depends on the situation in which it takes place. In Lave and Wenger's work, the mind as an independent factor, stripped of its context, has no power in explaining learning activities.[4]

The authors describe a variety of communities of practice, and through case histories and examples they show how newcomers learn from others as they move towards full participation in the social and cultural practices of a community.[5] The learning process in those communities can be generalized and applied to other social groups.

By focusing on the social context of learning, *Situated Learning* is an attempt to clarify the concept of apprenticeship—the centuries-old practice of learning a trade or profession through on-the-job training, under the supervision of an experienced practitioner or master. Prior to the book's publication, the term "apprenticeship" had been broadly used in learning studies without any solid theoretical understanding of what it meant, how it affected learning, and in what ways it differed from cognitive forms of learning. The authors sought to develop a coherent theory of apprenticeship, beyond the basic master–apprentice relationship.

Although the book was directed at an audience interested in apprenticeship theories, it touched off discussions among learning scholars from other disciplines, ranging from management theory to healthcare and public sector research. The book was found to be more broadly relevant than the authors anticipated.[6]

Why Does *Situated Learning* Matter?

Lave and Wenger's book introduces a new way of looking at how people acquire knowledge. Their pioneering work stresses the importance of social relationships, and broadens the concept of learning beyond the focus on cognitive processes and the theories of knowledge that then defined the field.

Lave and Wenger describe their apprenticeship theory by observing different kinds of communities, among them: midwives, tailors, US Navy quartermasters* (who supervise supplies), meat cutters, and non-drinking alcoholics. People learn by joining these communities and participating in activities, at first as fringe players. To begin with, they perform real tasks, but generally are not responsible for the more important or difficult activities. As they learn the skills necessary to carry out basic tasks, they become more involved in the processes of the community, moving from the "legitimate peripheral participation"* of the book's subtitle into "full participation." The main argument is that learning should not be seen as an individual's acquisition of knowledge, but as a process of social participation. The nature of the situation significantly affects the process.

The focus is on the ways in which learning is "an evolving, continuously renewed set of relations."[7] In general, the book seeks to answer the broad question of what is learning and what are its parts. It advances beyond the conventional concept of learning as a process that occurs in the mind, where all learning depends on the individual's ability to acquire and master knowledge. The book also departs from the usual idea that knowledge is just a body of facts. It criticizes the assumption that knowledge can be thought of as a question of facts, and that the learner is simply an individual who works with, memorizes, and applies those facts.[8]

NOTES

1   Jean Lave, "Biography," accessed November 20, 2015, http://www.ischool. berkeley.edu/people/faculty/jeanlave.

2   "Jean Lave, Etienne Wenger and Communities of Practice," Infed.org, accessed November 20, 2015, http://infed.org/mobi/jean-lave-etienne-wenger-and-communities-of-practice/.

3   Jean Lave and Etienne Wenger, *Situated Learning: Legitimate Peripheral Participation* (Cambridge: Cambridge University Press, 1991).

4   Lave and Wenger, *Situated Learning*, 20.

5   Lave and Wenger, *Situated Learning*, 24.

6   Lave and Wenger, *Situated Learning*, 27.

7   Lave and Wenger, *Situated Learning*, 53.

8   Lave and Wenger, *Situated Learning*, 32.

SECTION 1
INFLUENCES

MODULE 1
THE AUTHOR AND THE HISTORICAL CONTEXT

KEY POINTS

- *Situated Learning* represents an advanced stage in the authors' theoretical approach to the field of thought and learning.

- Lave's social anthropological* background exposed the authors to different social contexts of learning.

- In Lave's *Cognition in Practice* (1988), she can be seen to abandon the cognitive* approach to the understanding of learning—an approach that focuses on the ways in which knowledge is produced "internally" through thought alone.

Why Read This Text?

Jean Lave and Etienne Wenger's *Situated Learning: Legitimate Peripheral Participation* contributes to a growing body of research that focuses on the social elements of human understanding, learning, and communication. The book explores the relationship between learning and the context in which it occurs (that is, the social situation), a concept called situated learning.* According to this approach, learning is achieved through participation in social situations rather than through cognitive processes.[1] The book's principal question concerns the social contexts in which learning take place.

The main goal of the work is to translate the notion of situated learning into a specific approach to learning. To this end, the concept of "legitimate peripheral participation"* is key. "This is the process by which a learner becomes part of a community of practice* through his or her participation in the actual work" of an expert.[2] "Community of practice" here refers to a "community of people who care about a

> **❝** Arguing in favor of a shift away from a theory of situated activity in which learning is reified [made real] as one kind of activity, and toward a theory of social practice in which learning is viewed as an aspect of all activity, has led us to consider how we are to think of our own practice. **❞**
>
> Jean Lave and Etienne Wenger, *Situated Learning: Legitimate Peripheral Participation*

particular domain"of knowledge and the activities they share to be effective in this domain.[3] The learner participates marginally at first, with limited access and responsibility in the product of the community. Legitimate peripheral participation is explored through analysis of five studies of apprenticeship,* where people learn by doing something under the supervision of a more experienced person. Because the studies come from a variety of social and cultural contexts, the book can also be read as a work of anthropology.*

Authors' Lives

Lave is a social anthropologist based at the University of California, specializing in social theory. Her work has looked into the social practice of learning, learners, and educational institutions. She was heavily influenced by the American psychologist*and educator John Dewey's* theoretical understanding of the ways in which learning was achieved through experience and social interaction. Other thinkers noted for their work in the development of children, such as the Russian psychologist Lev Vygotsky* and the Swiss psychologist Jean Piaget,* also influenced her.[4]

While Lave's educational background logically led to her interest in communities of practice,* Wenger's was not so clearly linked. He was a teacher who joined the California-based Institute for Research on Learning,* a nonprofit institution with aims perfectly described by its name, after earning a doctorate in artificial intelligence* from the University of California, Irvine ("artificial intelligence" refers to intelligent behavior exhibited by computers). He currently provides consultancy services focused on the development of communities of practice within organizations. Wenger is also a cofounder and director of CPsquare,*a body he describes as "a practitioner's community on communities of practice."[5]

Lave and Wenger's novel analysis, published originally in *Situated Learning* and then expanded in later works, made important contributions to the field of social practice.

Authors' Background

Lave's earlier work focused on psychological evaluation of the social context of learning. For example, *Everyday Cognition* (1984), coedited with psychologist Barbara Rogoff,* was rooted in the work of the psychologist Lev Vygotsky.

Although *Situated Learning* describes an advanced stage in the authors' work, their thinking continued to evolve after the book's publication in 1991. For Wenger, the concept of communities of practice was only partly explored in *Situated Learning*. He developed the concept further in his 1998 *Communities of Practice*, in terms of both academia and the work of practitioners. He then considered how to actively develop these communities in *Cultivating Communities of Practice: A Guide to Managing Knowledge* (2002). In effect, from 1998 onwards, he abandoned the notion of situated learning to focus on communities of practice.

Lave, meanwhile, later developed her work by adopting a historical approach, while continuing as a scholar in the field of situated learning with communities of practice as her focal point.

NOTES

1   Stephen Fox, "Situated Learning Theory versus Traditional Cognitive Learning Theory: Why Management Education Should Not Ignore Management Learning," *Systemic Practice and Action Research* 10, no. 6 (1997): 727–47.

2   "Jean Lave, Etienne Wenger and Communities of Practice," Infed.org, accessed November 20, 2015, http://infed.org/mobi/jean-lave-etienne-wenger-and-communities-of-practice.

3   "Communities of Practice," Infed.org.

4   Lev Semyonovich Vygotsky, *Mind in Society: The Development of Higher Psychological Processes* (Cambridge, MA: Harvard University Press, 1980); and Jean Piaget, *The Origins of Intelligence in Children* (New York: International Universities Press, 1952).

5   CPsquare, "Our Vision," accessed January 20, 2016, http://cpsquare.org/vision/.

MODULE 2
ACADEMIC CONTEXT

KEY POINTS

- Cognitive learning theory* asserts that humans generate knowledge in the mind by developing mental abilities such as knowledge acquisition, assimilation, analysis, reflection, and application of knowledge.

- Lave and Wegner built on the work of previous scholars to develop situated learning* theory, in which they highlight both the social context in which learning takes place and traditional cognitive learning processes.

- Lave abandoned the cognitive dimension of learning altogether when she authored *Cognition in Practice* (1988), which discusses the relationship between cognition and practice (activities).

The Work in its Context

Jean Lave and Etienne Wenger's *Situated Learning: Legitimate Peripheral Participation* builds on the work of scholars who had declared that the cognitive model is inadequate to explain many aspects of learning. According to cognitive learning theory, learning is a mental process occurring in the minds of individuals. It regards individuals as the center of learning, and focuses on the significance of individual psychology throughout the learning process.

In their 1981 book *The Psychology of Literacy*, the American psychologists Sylvia Scribner* and Michael Cole* argued that the cognitive* framework could not explain the literacy rates among tailors in the West African nation of Liberia who spoke the Vai* language.[1] Through their observations, they concluded that Vai literacy was not about gaining knowledge of how to read and write a particular

> ❝ Situated Learning now appears to be a transitory concept, a bridge, between a view according to which cognitive processes (and thus learning) are primary and a view according to which social practice is the primary, generative phenomenon, and learning is one of its characteristics. ❞
>
> Jean Lave and Etienne Wenger, *Situated Learning: Legitimate Peripheral Participation*

script but, rather, about learning tailoring through practice.

Scribner and Cole's work is closely related to contemporary debates about the nature of learning. They wholeheartedly disagree with purely cognitive accounts of learning, and propose a shift in focus from mind and individuals to practice and communities. Notwithstanding criticism, this modification has led to new avenues for theories of learning in which practice plays a more important role than the mind. In Lave and Wenger's work, the mind as an independent factor has no power in explaining learning activities.

Overview of the Field

Lave and Wenger build on the work of their predecessors, particularly the Finnish educator Yrjö Engeström* and the Russian psychologist Lev Vygotsky,* who described human learning as a mental process of gathering knowledge and strengthening connections in the brain. According to this approach, learning occurs through a logical, step-by-step process, each step building a more sophisticated relationship between the person and the knowledge.

The steps are:

- Knowledge acquisition (getting the basic information)
- Assimilation (fitting the new information into the structure of the individual's existing experience and knowledge)

- Analysis
- Reflection
- Application (making use of the knowledge).

The British sociologist Anthony Giddens* and the French sociologist Pierre Bourdieu,* meanwhile, looked to the role of social structure* (ways of understanding a society in terms of the interaction between the different social groups that constitute it) and agency* (the ability of a person, or "agent," to act independently) in understanding why people act the way they do.[2] Lave and Wenger combine the learning processes of the cognitive camp and the notions of social structure and agency of the sociology camp, and propose a new contribution to learning theory based on social practice, participation, and the identity* of the individual.

Having invited researchers and established scholars with varying expertise to carry out research on learning, the Institute of Research on Learning* in Palo Alto, California, where Wenger was a researcher, was instrumental in shaping the ideas of *Situated Learning*.

Academic Influences

The authors come from different backgrounds with respect to the influences on the text. Lave was already an established social anthropologist,* having conducted many studies of apprenticeship in different parts of the world. She was invited to the Institute of Research on Learning during her sabbatical from the University of Chicago.

Wenger had a background in artificial intelligence,* with a master's degree in information and computer science and a doctorate in artificial intelligence from the University of California, Irvine. Much of the book is rooted in Lave's apprenticeship accounts, which led her to turn away from traditional cognitive learning theory and move toward social models of learning. Lave's previous book, *Cognition in*

Practice (1988), focuses on the relationship between cognition and practices. These contributions can be said to have paved the way for the change from cognitive learning theories to an understanding of learning through participating in a community of practice—a community dedicated to transmitting a particular domain of knowledge through the activities that define it.

NOTES

1   Sylvia Scribner and Michael Cole, *The Psychology of Literacy* (Cambridge, MA: Harvard University Press, 1981).

2   Anthony Giddens, *The Constitution of Society: Outline of the Theory of Structuration* (Cambridge: Polity Press, 1984); and Pierre Bourdieu, *Outline of a Theory of Practice*, trans. Richard Nice (Cambridge: Cambridge University Press, 1977).

MODULE 3
THE PROBLEM

KEY POINTS

- Lave and Wenger's book seeks to answer the broader question regarding the definition and constituent parts of learning.

- Before the publication of *Situated Learning,* most argued that cognitive* mental processes were highly beneficial and necessary components of learning.

- Lave and Wenger turned to cognitive psychology* (roughly, the way that knowledge is gained through mental processes) and the study of social structure and agency* (the individual's ability to act independently) to expand the notion of learning; to this end they focused on the social context of action, participation, and identity.*

Core Question

The central feature of Jean Lave and Etienne Wenger's *Situated Learning: Legitimate Peripheral Participation* regards the social context providing the proper setting for learning to take place.

Before the publication of *Situated Learning,* other works such as the Russian psychologist Lev Vygotsky's* *Mind in Society* (1979) had attempted to advance our understanding of learning and its relationship with the social context. Lave herself had explored cognitive learning theories from a social anthropological* perspective in the book she coedited with the psychologist Barbara Rogoff,* *Everyday Cognition* (1984).[1] This book, focusing on education and everyday activities, emphasizes the importance of the context in which thinking takes place. Lave's own book *Cognition in Practice* (1988) discusses the relationship between cognition and practice.[2]

❝ In reality, however, participation in social practice
… suggests a very explicit focus on the person, but
as person-in-the world, as member of a sociocultural
community. This focus in turn promotes a view of
knowing as activity by specific people in specific
circumstances. ❞

Jean Lave and Etienne Wenger, *Situated Learning: Legitimate Peripheral Participation*

Lave and Wenger's significant contribution lies in their proposing an account of social learning rooted in the ideas of apprenticeship,* or on-the-job training, that would go beyond the basic idea that learning is simply a question of acquiring knowledge. The text is noteworthy in offering a theoretical approach to apprenticeship that seeks to identify the processes through which learning occurs. The work also departs from the usual idea of knowledge as a body of abstract objects (that is, a system of facts); as Lave and Wenger's critical analysis seeks to prove, learning is not simply a matter of an individual memorizing and applying acquired facts.[3]

The Participants

Before Lave and Wenger wrote *Situated Learning*, the cognitive school of thought was dominant. This approach focused on learning as a mental process occurring in an individual's mind. Vygotsky and Jean Piaget, a Swiss psychologist notable for his contribution to the theory of child development, were two prominent scholars in this field. Vygotsky's *Educational Psychology* (1926) and Piaget's *The Origins of Intelligence in Children* (1936) asserted that human learning was essentially a series of internal steps. The individual acquired facts and assimilated them (that is, fitted them into his or her existing knowledge); he or she analyzed and reflected on the facts and, finally, applied the new knowledge gained. Learning, then, was largely a mental process of internalizing knowledge that strengthened connections in the brain.[4]

Sociologists such as Anthony Giddens* and Pierre Bourdieu* took a different approach, in which society was key. According to their social theory, an individual's actions developed through a combination of social structure and agency.[5] Giddens argued that social structures both cause, and are caused by, people's daily activities. As a result, one cannot exist without the other. Giddens shares Bourdieu's understanding that practice plays a vital role in human social structures. By combining the social context of Giddens and Bourdieu with learning from cognitive theorists such as Piaget, Lave and Wenger introduced a learning theory that was based on social practice, participation, and the identity of the individual.

The Contemporary Debate

When Lave and Wenger wrote the text they were based at the Institute for Research on Learning,* an institution founded with the aim of understanding the processes and locations through and in which learning takes place. The Institute was based at PARC (the Palo Alto Research Center), a research facility instrumental in the development of much modern communications and computer technology. During their time at the Institute there was a growing interest in apprenticeship as a learning device, but no theoretical framework for examining precisely how apprenticeship enabled learning. Their book aimed to fill this gap.

The authors were guided by their own respective studies. Lave's previous work around craft apprenticeship in West Africa and Wenger's background in artificial intelligence* were also significant. They cite the influential American anthropologist* Brigitte Jordan's* work dealing with midwives on the Yucatan peninsula in Mexico—work that led to Lave and Wenger coining the term "communities of practice."* Based on Jordan's studies, Lave and Wenger describe how, over a period of many years, Yucatec midwives moved from being peripheral to full participants in the midwifery community (the process described as "legitimate peripheral participation"* in the book's subtitle.) In doing so, they demonstrate that apprenticeship occurs as a way of life and that the acquisition of knowledge is a byproduct of being part of the community.

The authors propose a learning theory according to which learning is more than simply a question of "doing." They see situated learning* (learning taking place in a specific place) as an ongoing activity in our social lives. This line of thinking ultimately paved the way for the introduction of the concept of legitimate peripheral participation.

NOTES

1   Barbara Rogoff and Jean Lave, eds, *Everyday Cognition: Its Development in Social Context* (Cambridge, MA: Harvard University Press, 1984).

2   Jean Lave, *Cognition in Practice: Mind, Mathematics and Culture in Everyday Life* (Cambridge: Cambridge University Press, 1988).

3   Jean Lave and Etienne Wenger, *Situated Learning: Legitimate Peripheral Participation* (Cambridge: Cambridge University Press, 1991), 42.

4   Lev Semyonovich Vygotsky, *Educational Psychology* (Cambridge, MA: MIT, 1926); and Jean Piaget, *The Origins of Intelligence in Children* (New York: International University Press, 1952).

5   Anthony Giddens, *The Constitution of Society: Outline of the Theory of Structuration* (Cambridge: Polity Press, 1984); and Pierre Bourdieu, *Outline of a Theory of Practice*, trans. Richard Nice (Cambridge: Cambridge University Press, 1977).

MODULE 4
THE AUTHOR'S CONTRIBUTION

KEY POINTS

- Lave and Wenger's primary aim in *Situated Learning* is to clarify the theory and concept of apprenticeship.*

- Through five case studies of apprenticeship the authors contribute to learning theories by introducing the concept of legitimate peripheral participation*—the process by which those with little experience in a field come to play an important role through practice.

- *Situated Learning* combined and built upon previous work on cognitive psychology,* social structures,* and agency* in order to propose a genuine contribution to learning theory.

Authors' Aims

The main aim of Jean Lave and Etienne Wenger's *Situated Learning: Legitimate Peripheral Participation* was to expand on the concept of apprenticeship as an important means of learning. Through their work at the Institute of Research on Learning* in California, the authors were motivated by a desire to move beyond the superficial understanding of apprenticeship (then something of a buzzword in learning studies). The authors were not fully convinced that the cognitive* school of thought, which emphasized the separation of mind and body, was a good model for learning. Instead, they sought an alternative approach that combined the mind and body with a social context of learning, based on observations of certain instances of apprenticeship.[1]

While the book clearly states that the authors' focus is the social context of learning, the text attracted some criticism regarding the apprenticeship cases. For example, the text argues that the concept of

❝ Arguing in favor of a shift away from a theory of situated activity in which learning is one kind of activity, and toward a theory of social practice in which learning is viewed as an aspect of all activity, has led us to consider how we are to think about our own practice. ❞

Jean Lave and Etienne Wenger, *Situated Learning: Legitimate Peripheral Participation*

legitimate peripheral participation* is better than conventional schooling theories. It does not compare cases of schooling and apprenticeship, however, mostly citing practical examples from apprenticeship.[2]

Several questions remain unanswered: Is apprenticeship a better form of learning? If so, why? How were the examples of apprenticeship chosen? Were the cases selected because they illustrated legitimate peripheral participation? Nevertheless, although the book can be considered flawed, the authors seem to be clear and focused in keeping to their original intention to develop a theory of apprenticeship.

Approach

In discussing legitimate peripheral participation, the authors describe actual cases of apprenticeship. All of the studies and examples illustrate a complex system of learning rooted in the relations between newcomers and old-timers* (experienced and accepted members) in various communities, examining their history, technology, and career paths.

The five accounts of apprenticeship include:

- Midwives in Mexico who speak Yucatec Mayan*
- Tailors in the West African nation of Liberia who speak the Vai* language and belong to the Gola clothes-crafting community

- Quartermasters* in the US Navy- men responsible for administering supplies
- Butchers in American supermarkets
- Non-drinking alcoholics in Alcoholics Anonymous*

The cases vary in the forms of apprenticeship and the degree to which apprenticeship is integrated into social life.[3] The examples inspire the authors to illuminate the nature of learning within the wider cultural and political context.

Lave and Wenger justify their arguments by:

- Presenting their ideas
- Contrasting them with existing assumptions
- Supporting their views by empirical* evidence (evidence verifiable by observation)
- Elaborating on their framework of learning by answering the challenges raised in the course of analyzing the cases.

Contribution in Context

Lave and Wenger were not the first to describe the concept of legitimate peripheral participation. Scholars such as the Russian psychologist Lev Vygotsky* and the Helsinki-based educational theorist Yrjö Engeström* spoke about the "zone of proximal development"*—the difference between what a learner can learn without any help and what he or she can learn with help.[4]

Lave and Wenger's principal contribution, then, is marrying this concept with social structures and practice to inform a theory of apprenticeship. They consider how it affects learning, and in what ways it is different from cognitive forms of learning. The authors depart from the conventional idea of learning as an individual-driven process in which the mind determines learning and all learning depends on the individual's ability to acquire and master knowledge.

Their work also departs from the idea that knowledge is a body of facts. It criticizes the detachment of factual statements from the learner who works with, memorizes, and applies those facts.

NOTES

1   Jean Lave and Etienne Wenger, *Situated Learning: Legitimate Peripheral Participation* (Cambridge: Cambridge University Press, 1991), 59.

2   Lave and Wenger, *Situated Learning*, 89.

3   Brigitte Jordan, "Cosmopolitical Obstetrics: Some Insights from the Training of Traditional Midwives," *Social Science & Medicine* 28, no. 9 (1989): 925–37.

4   Yrjö Engeström, *Developmental Work Research: Expanding Activity Theory in Practice* (Berlin: Lehmanns Media, 2005), 154, f.3.

SECTION 2
IDEAS

MODULE 5
MAIN IDEAS

KEY POINTS

- *Situated Learning* argues that communities of practice* provide a powerful context for learning through apprenticeship—a key aspect of what the authors describe as "legitimate peripheral participation."*

- Lave and Wenger contend that all learning is situated learning*—that is, learning always depends on the learner's situation and relationship with other learners.

- Although the writing is dense, *Situated Learning* provides a wealth of concepts and examples from case studies of five communities of practice.

Key Themes

Put simply, the theory Jean Lave and Etienne Wenger develop in their book *Situated Learning: Legitimate Peripheral Participation* (1991) goes as follows. A community of practice is a group of people with similar interests, perspectives and activities. In such a community, newcomers learn from "old-timers"* by participating in the community; this process is called legitimate peripheral participation. As newcomers develop understanding and knowledge they move from the periphery of the community to the core, ultimately becoming old-timers themselves.[1]

The book presents the idea that learning through legitimate peripheral participation depends on the opportunities newcomers are given for learning through practice, rather than learning through supervision by an instructor or master who may be too distant to learn from. Instead the newcomer learns from peers, based on the opportunities provided by social structures. Hence, learning is embedded in participation opportunities and levels of engagement.

> **❝** Our initial intention in writing what has gradually evolved into this book was to rescue the idea of apprenticeship. **❞**
>
> Jean Lave and Etienne Wenger, *Situated Learning: Legitimate Peripheral Participation*

Exploring the Ideas

Lave and Wenger argue that there is no learning that is not situated—that learning is always affected by the situation of the learner, and by his or her level of engagement and relationship with other learners. According to the authors, learning occurs most effectively within a community of practice. This is a departure from traditional cognitive learning theory,* according to which learning takes place entirely within an individual's mind. Lave and Wenger's work represents a fundamental shift in the underlying assumptions about how learning occurs, and emphasizes the importance of the relations between various parts of the social world.[2]

Early in the book, the authors offer an unsatisfying discussion of why they chose the words that form their concept of legitimate peripheral participation. "Peripheral participation" is a fairly straightforward term, but why did they choose "legitimate" as opposed to "beneficial," or "instructive," or some other positive term? As the authors write, "In the terms proposed here there may very well be no such thing as an 'illegitimate peripheral participant' ... legitimate peripherality is a complex notion [that can describe] a place in which one is kept from participating more fully—often legitimately, from the broader perspective of society at large."[3]

Situated Learning uses five case studies to illustrate the varying nature of the community of practice and legitimate peripheral participation. Each case focuses on different ways in which old-timers and newcomers establish and maintain competing viewpoints on the practice and its development. On the one hand, newcomers need to engage in existing practice in order to understand, participate, and to become full members of the community. On the other hand, they have a stake in the development of their communities as they begin to establish their own identity.*[4]

Language and Expression

Although there have been concerns about the density of the text, stylistically speaking *Situated Learning* is rich in useful concepts and examples taken from diverse apprenticeship settings to illustrate the authors' ideas and explanations. Through five varied case studies, the authors explore how people move from being novice learners on the periphery of a community of practice to becoming seasoned, cultured practitioners able to share knowledge with new learners.

The authors wrote the book for a readership interested in apprenticeship theories, which were then becoming popular. Despite its dense writing, the book attracted interest beyond its intended audience, and kindled a new dialogue between learning scholars and other academic disciplines.

NOTES

1   Jean Lave and Etienne Wenger, *Situated Learning: Legitimate Peripheral Participation* (Cambridge: Cambridge University Press, 1991), 53.

2   Lave and Wenger, *Situated Learning*, 52.

3   Lave and Wenger, Situated Learning, 35–6.

4   Lave and Wenger, *Situated Learning*, 36.

MODULE 6
SECONDARY IDEAS

KEY POINTS

- Lave and Wenger discuss three secondary themes that challenge conventional theories of learning: internalization* (an individual's acceptance of norms and values established by others), the construction of identity,* and the development of communities of practice.*

- These themes all relate to the process of newcomers evolving into old-timers*—a process they term "legitimate peripheral participation."*

- Lave and Wenger also engage in a brief discussion about identity and power dynamics in aspects of the learning process in communities of practice.

Other Ideas

In *Situated Learning: Legitimate Peripheral Participation*, Lave and Wenger challenge conventional theories of learning by exploring the three ideas of internalization, construction of identity, and the development of communities of practice. They first question the concept of internalization, an idea that had already been widely developed in literature that dealt with learning. Internalization is based on the notion that a person accepts the standards and principles that others have founded. Lave and Wenger raise key questions about the definition of what is "internal" and what is "external" in the social world and the extent to which internalization is a universal—or common—process. They also discuss how the process of learning within the community of practice itself becomes a form of identity building. The transformation of identity from novice to master is what lies beneath the learning process within the community.

" We gradually became convinced that we needed to reexamine ... historical forms of apprenticeship. This led us to insist on the distinction between our theoretical framework for analyzing educational forms and specific historical instances of apprenticeship. This in turn led us to explore learning as situated learning. "

Jean Lave and Etienne Wenger, *Situated Learning: Legitimate Peripheral Participation*

If we appreciate that it is easier to understand this kind of community in terms of the *practice* rather than the *identities* that define it, and that it is easier for researchers to *observe* practice than to *measure* identity, then it is possible to think that discussion of identity is really not enough.

Exploring the Ideas

Some authors have provided satisfactory explanations and evidence based on experience about the way identities can affect learning.[1] However, it was not until Lave and Wenger's own later works— Wenger's *Communities of Practice* (1998), for example—that a proper theory of learning and identity was developed further. In that text, Wenger focuses on the way in which identities are formed and also negotiated in the community of practice.[2]

For communities of practice to be able to develop, there needs to be a process that will allow newcomers to become part of the community. Access is granted not only by the master, but by other apprentices who are themselves already part of the community of practice. As the master may be too distant to learn from, the newcomer learns from peers through the opportunities provided by social relations, interests, and power relations. The peers, meanwhile, collectively ask questions about whether the apprentice is competent to move into more sophisticated areas of the practice. But does the rest of the community accept these claims of the newcomer's competence? And is the master challenged by both the apprentice and by the claims? Answers to these questions will address the way members build legitimacy within the community, and will highlight the differences in power between its members.[3]

Overlooked

Although *Situated Learning* discusses the idea and the influence of power in passing, it is true that this this is not one of the book's central themes—and it is not expressly developed within the text.[4] Before *Situated Learning* first appeared in 1991, theories of power were developed entirely separately from theories of learning. Even though Lave and Wenger only briefly highlight the existence and the nature of power relationships between old-timers and newcomers in communities of practice, by doing so the authors at least managed to suggest there is a need for a more comprehensive theory of learning. This deeper, newer theory needs to take into consideration the political dimension of learning, particularly where power is concerned. It is highly likely that communities of practice exist where the community is weakened because certain types of power relationships act as a barrier either to entry to the group in the first place, or to useful later participation in that group. In his own later works, Wenger himself acknowledges the importance of the role of power in learning.[5]

NOTES

1   Anna Sfard and Anna Prusak, "Telling Identities: In Search of an Analytic Tool for Investigating Learning as a Culturally Shaped Activity," *Educational Researcher* 34, no. 4 (2005): 14–22.

2   Etienne Wenger, *Communities of Practice: Learning, Meaning, and Identity* (Cambridge: Cambridge University Press, 1998).

3   Dorothy Holland, *Identity and Agency in Cultural Worlds* (Cambridge, MA: Harvard University Press, 2001).

4   Jean Lave and Etienne Wenger, *Situated Learning: Legitimate Peripheral Participation* (Cambridge: Cambridge University Press, 1991), 54.

5   Wenger, *Communities of Practice*.

MODULE 7
ACHIEVEMENT

KEY POINTS

- Lave and Wenger's *Situated Learning* has been influential in shaping, directing, and defining research and practice on the development of learning theories.

- The authors do not discuss the widely varied nature of communities of practice,* leading to confusion about the concept and its application to the real world.

- Critics argue that the text is historically and culturally bounded, and less relevant in the contemporary world.

Assessing the Argument

Jean Lave and Etienne Wenger's primary objective when writing *Situated Learning: Legitimate Peripheral Participation* was to clarify the theory of apprenticeship.* The text remains focused on exploring the social context of learning. Despite initial skepticism from learning theorists, the authors' work is widely recognized not only by educational scholars, but in the field of developmental studies (the study of the acquisition of knowledge and the formation of the personality), organizational studies (the study of the nature and functioning of organizations), healthcare management, and the development of new technology. More than 20 years after its 1991 publication, the book is still widely cited by practitioners and academics. For example, researchers have investigated how external events affect situated learning through case studies of technical after-sales services. The context of communities of practice has also been applied within settings of the management of organizational change. Similarly, in healthcare, there have been a number of attempts to

> **❝** Lave and Wenger, with their concept of legitimate peripheral participation (LPP), provide one of the most versatile accounts of this constructive view of learning. LPP, it must quickly be asserted, is not a method of education. It is an analytical category or tool for understanding learning across different methods, different historical periods, and different social and physical environments. **❞**
>
> John Seely Brown and Paul Duguid, "Organizational Learning and Communities-of-Practice: Toward a Unified View of Working, Learning, and Innovation," *Organization Science*

cultivate communities of practice for the transfer of knowledge between researchers and the clinicians who directly treat patients.[1]

Achievement in Context

Lave and Wenger propose "a new approach to understanding learning, including that which takes place in the workplace."[2] They focus on informal and situated social interaction, rather than on traditional forms of knowledge-sharing such as lectures, workshops, and solitary reading. "Such interaction achieves authentic, motivated learning of what needs to be known about the complexities of real practice."[3] The central logic of the book is that learning is more than the acquisition of knowledge; it requires a change in identity,* which occurs through participation in the community of practice.

The concept of the community of practice has proved to be quite flexible, molding to fit various disciplines. Organizational researchers have used the concept as a practical tool to advance learning. Their priority is to explore how to build or cultivate communities of practice that can function across various boundaries. Lave and Wenger's explanations of the process of learning have become crucially important to the field of education studies.

Nonetheless, there are certain issues around the narrow idea of the learning process as set out by the authors. Not every social setting is arranged in a way that can support the community of practice, especially today when members of organizations are often classified by rank, and communication occurs exclusively online. Because the work has its roots in studies of apprenticeship in less well-developed societies, some have argued that it takes a backward step by ignoring institutions and practices that have improved modern education. Moreover, the book's model of legitimate peripheral participation* takes place over long periods of time; this might not be practical in some business settings, where speed of learning is crucial in the evaluation of the achievements of individuals and organizations.[4]

Limitations

Several questions have puzzled researchers in real-world studies, such as how the actual site of learning should be understood in the light of wider issues of social and economic inequalities. What is the relationship between power, in the sense of social status, and access to learning? How do we measure or observe communities of practice? How do we determine who is at the core and who at the periphery? And where are the boundaries?

Situated Learning's popularity has led to it being used by different groups to suit different needs, adding further confusion to its core ideas. For example, workplace-learning theorists use the concept of communities of practice as a homogenous (that is, internally alike) entity, without considering any of the relationships within the community.

In developing a coherent theory of apprenticeship beyond the superficial master–apprentice relationship, the authors remain primarily focused on illustrating the case of communities of practice. However, there has been criticism of some of their methods and examples. The authors do not compare the differences between cases of schooling and cases of apprenticeship with empirical evidence. It is, therefore, uncertain whether apprenticeship is indeed a better form of learning. How and why were the cases of apprenticeship chosen? Was it just for their value in illustrating legitimate peripheral learning? For all of these reasons, the book can be considered somewhat flawed.[5]

NOTES

1   Jon Erland Lervik et al., "Temporal Dynamics of Situated Learning in Organizations," *Management Learning* 41, no. 3 (2010): 285–301.

2   Andrew Cox, "What Are Communities of Practice? A Comparative Review of Four Seminal Works," *Journal of Information* Science 31, no. 6 (2005): 527–40.

3   Cox, "What Are Communities of Practice?" 527–40.

4   Enrique Murillo, "Communities of Practice in the Business and Organization Studies Literature," *Information Research* 16, no. 1 (2011): 1.

5   Phil Hodkinson and Heather Hodkinson. "A Constructive Critique of Communities of Practice: Moving Beyond Lave and Wenger," *OVAL Research Working Paper* (2004).

MODULE 8
PLACE IN THE AUTHOR'S WORK

KEY POINTS

- Lave's background as a social anthropologist* helped pave the way for a new model of learning focusing on the social context in which learning takes place.

- Following the publication of *Situated Learning*, Wenger extended the idea of communities of practice* in his second book, *Communities of Practice* (1998).

- *Situated Learning* made a significant impact not just with scholars but also with learning organizations and learning communities outside of academia.

Positioning

In 1991, when Jean Lave and Etienne Wenger wrote *Situated Learning: Legitimate Peripheral Participation*, Lave was already an established social anthropologist with an interest in the social context of cognition* (roughly, the relationship between society and thought); Wenger was a junior researcher, working in the discipline of artificial intelligence.* Considering education and everyday activities, and emphasizing the importance of context in thought, the book reflects Lave's previous research interests. Her earlier work *Cognition in Practice* (1988), for example, discusses the relationship between cognition and practice, viewing cognition as a process that differs from person to person, depending on the individual's experience and situation.[1]

Although *Situated Learning* is rooted in Lave's anthropological background, Wenger played an essential role in the development of the theory. Later he took the concept of communities of practice* and made it his own, developing a deeper and richer understanding for both practitioners and scholars.

66 The concept of community of practice does not exist by itself. It is part of a broader conceptual framework for thinking about learning in its social dimensions. **99**

Etienne Wenger, *Communities of Practice and Social Learning Systems*

The combined contributions of the two authors paved the way for the shift in focus from cognitive psychology to social anthropology. The book represents a consolidation of arguments already established by other scholars as well as by Lave herself.

Wenger joined the Institute of Research on Learning* at Palo Alto following his research in artificial intelligence. Lave, being a social anthropologist, was an intellectually disruptive force at the Institute because of her conviction that the chief factor affecting behavior is an individual's immediate situation. The theory of situated learning was the product of this creative, interdisciplinary mix.

Integration

Situated Learning describes an advanced stage in Lave's theoretical approach to learning development. Not until writing it did she finally abandon an approach to learning theory founded on cognition, by committing to the principle that social context was more important to the acquisition of knowledge than the invisible processes of the mind. However, while striking a mature note, it does not represent the final, fully developed stage of her thinking.

The same can be said of Wenger, then at the start of his career. In his subsequent work, Wenger took the concept of communities of practice and developed it further both in practitioners' environments and in academia. For example, in 1998 he published *Communities of Practice: Learning, Meaning, and Identity*, in which he extended the theory of the community of practice to include contexts where situated learning (or legitimate peripheral participation*) took place;

his aim was to examine how these communities evolved and how they could be cultivated.

Later, Wenger appeared to have abandoned the notion of situated learning to focus on the community of practice, while Lave continued as a scholar in the field of situated learning.[2] The concept has been enriched, developing into a practical, real-world tool for learning (especially in Wenger's work) and focusing on the ways in which identity*is formed in the learning process, rather than the means by which participation occurs.

Significance

Lave and Wenger's theory of apprenticeship and notions of the community of practice have made a significant impact on organizations and learning communities. Their work has been most influential in the field of organizational development (the process by which organizations develop.) The apprenticeship model connected strongly with important schools of thought regarding training and development within organizations.

More significantly, the growing interest in the organization as a body capable of developing by acquiring knowledge through the development of informal networks and groupings has been a useful addition to the concept of the community of practice. It meant that communities of practice were regarded as valuable assets. The importance of the community of practice was not only widely recognized by educational scholars but also by those within the field of developmental and healthcare studies.

NOTES

1   Jean Lave, *Cognition in Practice: Mind, Mathematics and Culture in Everyday Life* (Cambridge: Cambridge University Press, 1988).

2   Dorothy Holland and Jean Lave, "Social Practice Theory and the Historical Production of Persons," *Actio: An International Journal of Human Activity Theory* 2 (2009): 1–15.

SECTION 3
IMPACT

MODULE 9
THE FIRST RESPONSES

KEY POINTS

- *Situated Learning* was criticized for the authors' method and for its imprecisions; in addition, its relevance to the modern world was challenged.

- To a large extent, Wenger's essay "Communities of Practice and Social Learning Systems" is a response to the criticisms leveled at *Situated Learning.*

- In expanding the response, Wenger says that although online networks are replacing communities to some degree, each model has value and can address the other's shortcomings.

Criticism

In general, the critics have focused on three areas concerning Jean Lave and Etienne Wenger's *Situated Learning: Legitimate Peripheral Participation*: the ambiguities of their concepts; the lack of empirical* evidence to support their case; and the questionable aptness of the concept in the modern digital age.

The social theorists Alessia Contu* and Hugh Willmott,* both interested in matters relating to organizations, complain that the social context of learning as defined by Lave and Wenger does not clarify which social theory they are drawing from.[1] Social theory has been developed in different ways. This has led some thinkers to disregard the notion of learning through apprenticeship,* as the text does not discuss the dynamics of conflict between newcomers and old-timers.* Lave and Wenger largely ignore the notion of power, leaving it to the Swedish business administration scholar Lars Lindkvist* and other researchers to explore the power dynamics within and between communities of power.[2]

❝ The concept of community of practice does not exist by itself. It is part of a broader conceptual framework for thinking about learning in its social dimensions. It is a perspective that locates learning, not in the head or outside it, but in the relationship between the person and the world, which for human beings is a social person in a social world. In this relation of participation, the social and the individual constitute each other. **❞**

Etienne Wenger, "Communities of Practice and Social Learning Systems: The Career of a Concept"

Similarly, the British social scientist Jason Hughes* and his coauthors complained that, though Lave and Wenger provide a general definition of the community of practice, the precise meaning of the term is not clear.[3] The reader is left to speculate about what exactly is meant.

In spite of the use of case studies to provide empirical evidence, the British administration scholar Joanne Roberts* has called the authors' methodology (the methods used in the gathering and interpretation of research) inadequate.[4] The cases provided in the book hardly touch on political and historical aspects of legitimate peripheral participation, but simply demonstrate how newcomers become old-timers in the organizations studied.

The US education scholar Christine Greenhow* has argued that the community of practice model does not fit well in the modern digital world.[5] Similarly, the Australian education scholars Jan Herrington* and Ron Oliver* note that online communities and social networks often have vague boundaries or none at all, which undercuts the existence of the community of practice as argued by Lave and Wenger.[6]

Responses

Wenger replied to the critiques by addressing three major aspects of the community of practice: power, the implications of the digital age, and the divide between the community of practice as a real-world phenomenon and as an analytical concept.

By establishing the community of practice as a learning theory, rather than as a political theory, Wenger emphasizes that power relations in these communities—the ways in which differences in social status are perceived—are founded on claims to competence.[7] Learning and power are interrelated. Furthermore, Eivor Oborn* and Sandra Dawson,* scholars interested in the field of organization, both point to the ways in which fields of practice overlap in a manner that might cause conflicts.[8]

As for the modern age of technology, Wenger notes a tendency for communities, in which individual identity* plays a vital role, to be replaced by networks that are based on connectivity. He says that pairing the two models can enable each to overcome the other's weaknesses. A community that is too tight can result in group-thinking—an echo-chamber effect. On the other hand, a network that is too loose can undermine opportunities to act collectively, as it will be highly individualized.[9]

Further, Wenger believes that the idea of the community of practice is a useful tool in both analytical and real-world terms. As an analytical tool, the community of practice helps to analyze and understand *how learning takes place* (the transfer of knowledge from old-timers to newcomers, for example). As a real-world tool, the community of practice is *part of the learning process itself*, helping to explain or predict the effect of community dynamics in different contexts. In their later works, Lave and Wenger clarify the definition of the community of practice and make a distinction between the analytical and empirical (real-world) uses of the concept.[10]

Conflict and Consensus

Situated Learning has reshaped social-learning theories by eliminating the separation of mind and body, focusing on the social world. Wenger's later works have looked at boundaries between communities of practice, the ways the boundaries can be crossed, and their impact on learning. The idea that situation and context are inseparable from learning has gained broad acceptance by scholars, including the leadership and ethics scholar Bruce Kogut* and the business strategy and management scholar Udo Zander.*[11]

In addition, the book has inspired other developments in the field of learning theory and organizational studies, such as research into the importance of identity and narrative. Though *Situated Learning* does not present itself as a radical and novel contribution, it has revolutionized academic understanding of the impact of social systems on learning.

NOTES

1   Alessia Contu and Hugh Willmott, "Re-Embedding Situatedness: The Importance of Power Relations in Learning Theory," *Organization Science* 14, no. 3 (2003): 283–96.

2   Lars Lindkvist, "Knowledge Communities and Knowledge Collectivities: A Typology of Knowledge Work in Groups," *Journal of Management Studies* 42, no. 6 (2005):1196.

3   Jason Hughes et al., eds, *Communities of Practice: Critical Perspectives* (London: Routledge, 2007).

4   Joanne Roberts, "Limits to Communities of Practice," *Journal of Management Studies* 43, no. 3 (2006): 623–39.

5   Christine Greenhow et al., "Learning, Teaching, and Scholarship in a Digital Age: Web 2.0 and Classroom Research—What Path Should We Take 'Now'?" *Educational Researcher* 38, no. 4 (2009): 246–59.

6   Jan Herrington and Ron Oliver, "Critical Characteristics of Situated Learning: Implications for the Instructional Design of Multimedia," murdoch.edu.au

(1995), accessed April 5, 2016, http://researchrepository.murdoch.edu.
au/7189/1/critical_characteristics.pdf.

7   Etienne Wenger, "Communities of Practice and Social Learning Systems:
The Career of a Concept," in *Social Learning Systems and Communities of
Practice*, ed. Chris Blackmore (London: Springer, 2010): 180.

8   Eivor Oborn and Sandra Dawson, "Learning across Communities of
Practice: An Examination of Multidisciplinary Work," *British Journal of
Management* 21, no. 4 (2010): 843–58.

9   Wenger, "Communities of Practice and Social Learning Systems," 185.

10 Wenger, "Communities of Practice and Social Learning Systems," 183.

11 Bruce Kogut and Udo Zander, "What Firms Do? Coordination, Identity, and
Learning," *Organization Science* 7, no. 5 (1996): 502–18.

MODULE 10
THE EVOLVING DEBATE

KEY POINTS

- Lave and Wenger's argument that learning occurs through legitimate peripheral participation* in communities of practice* was largely accepted.

- While their ideas do not rise to the level of a "school of thought" in social-learning theory, researchers often refer to a "situated learning"* approach.

- Lave and Wenger's text has been applied to various disciplines in the social sciences, including learning, education, organizational studies, healthcare, and developmental studies,* and to real-world business settings.

Uses and Problems

Jean Lave and Etienne Wenger's *Situated Learning: Legitimate Peripheral Participation* received a lot of attention in management studies, particularly from John Seely Brown,* an American researcher specializing in the impact of computer-supported activities on forms of learning, and Paul Duguid,* a scholar interested in the history of information who applied the concept of communities of practice in organizations for the first time.[1] Later, Wenger himself established a consultancy in response to the interest in communities of practice from business audiences.

Brown and Duguid developed their theory of the community of practice by focusing on differences between levels of experience and between different practices across organizations. As such, their focus is on how practices coordinate within organizations. By contrast, the scholars Wanda Orlikowski,* Silvia Gherardi,* and Davide Nicolini*

❝ Workplace learning is best understood, then, in terms of the communities being formed or joined and personal identities being changed. The central issue in learning is becoming a practitioner not learning about practice. This approach draws attention away from abstract knowledge and cranial processes and situates it in the practices and communities in which knowledge takes on significance. **❞**

John Seely Brown and Paul Duguid, "Organizational Learning and Communities of Practice: Toward a Unified View of Working, Learning and Innovation"

separately developed more general ideas of how knowledge is embedded in practice.[2]

Recent studies have developed and explored the launching and managing of the community of practice; how such communities shape the identities of participants; and the virtual (online) community of practice.[3] Some authors have discussed whether and how a new community of practice can be launched, and what can be done to manage and control it once it has been created.[4] Others have examined how the communities' boundaries lead to innovation.[5] Wenger himself describes social-learning systems as having multiple communities of practice with multiple boundaries.[6]

Schools of Thought

Situated Learning has inspired further developments in the field of learning theories. A large part of the intellectual debate about knowledge in the activity theory* formulated by the Finland-based scholar Yrjö Engeström,* and in the figured worlds theory* of social scientist Dorothy Holland,* has its roots in Lave and Wenger's text. (Activity theory describes the role of structure and division of labor in learning[7]; figured worlds theory explores the role of narratives and stories in the development of cultural worlds.)

Both situated learning* and activity theory attempt to form theoretical frameworks that consider learning and thinking to be integral aspects of practice in a social, cultural, and material world. Moreover, both attempt to include notions of history, development, transitions, and change into their theoretical frameworks. They also emphasize that human activity is affected by tools, and that it sits in a social context. It is worth noting that although these strands were influenced by, and have influenced, the situated learning theory, they cannot be considered as originating from this text.

These theories form the base of a social theory of learning in which agency*—an individual's ability to act independently—plays a larger role than in the notion of situated learning. These recent developments have abandoned the term "situated learning" to underscore the relevance of agency in structures such as organizations and communities. This shift has opened new ground for research to explore the dynamics between practice, agency, and structure.

In Current Scholarship

Wenger continues to work as a researcher and consultant and has kept up with the development of the field following the publication of *Situated Learning*. He is still focused, through both research and consultancy with business organizations, on exploring social-learning systems. He continues to argue that there are connections among knowledge, community, learning, and identity.

The main thrust of his work is that human knowledge is gained through social interactions. His subsequent books, such as *Communities of Practice: Learning, Meaning, and Identity* (1998), lay out a theory of learning based on the concept; *Digital Habitats* (2009) deals with the use of technology, and *Cultivating Communities of Practice: A Guide to Managing Knowledge* (2013) is aimed at practitioners.

Wenger's work in improving communities of practice has been a key feature of learning in a growing number of organizations in both the private and public sectors. His work has been influential in theory and practice in areas such as business, government, international development, healthcare, and education. By means of consulting, public speaking, and workshops, Wenger assists organizations in adopting the concept of communities of practice. He holds several key academic positions, such as a visiting professorship at the University of Manchester in the UK and the University of Aalborg in Denmark, and has been awarded an honorary doctorate from the University of Brighton in the UK.

NOTES

1   John Seely Brown and Paul Duguid, "Knowledge and Organization: A Social-Practice Perspective," *Organization Science* 12, no. 2 (2001): 198–213.

2   Wanda J. Orlikowski, "Knowing in Practice: Enacting a Collective Capability in Distributed Organizing," *Organization Science* 13, no. 3 (2002): 249–73; Silvia Gherardi, "Practice-Based Theorizing on Learning and Knowing in Organizations," *Organization* 7, no. 2 (2000): 211–23; and Silvia Gherardi and Davide Nicolini, "To Transfer is to Transform: The Circulation of Safety Knowledge," *Organization* 7, no. 2 (2000): 329–48.

3   John Seely Brown and Paul Duguid, "Organizational Learning and Communities-of-Practice: Toward a Unified View of Working, Learning, and Innovation," *Organization Science* 2, no.1 (1991): 40–57.

4   Line Dubé et al., "The Impact of Structuring Characteristics on the Launching of Virtual Communities of Practice," *Journal of Organizational Change Management* 18, no. 2 (2005): 145–66.

5   Patrice Braun, "Digital Knowledge Networks: Linking Communities of Practice with Innovation," *Journal of Business Strategies* 19, no. 1 (2002): 43.

6   Etienne Wenger, "Communities of Practice and Social Learning Systems: The Career of a Concept," in *Social Learning Systems and Communities of Practice*, ed. Chris Blackmore (London: Springer, 2010), 179–98.

7   Yrjö Engeström et al., *Perspectives on Activity Theory* (Cambridge: Cambridge University Press, 1999).

MODULE 11
IMPACT AND INFLUENCE TODAY

KEY POINTS

- *Situated Learning* remains a key text for anyone who is interested in understanding the process of learning, apprenticeship,* and communities of practice.*

- While theories of social learning* are mainly inspired by this work, empirical* research raises challenges to the concepts of situated learning.*

- The book's findings have been applied to the field of organizational studies, where the reaction has been generally positive, even if some skepticism exists from the author Lave herself.

Position

The ideas contained in Jean Lave and Etienne Wenger's *Situated Learning: Legitimate Peripheral Participation* were adopted early on by practitioners in business. The US technology company Xerox funded the Institute for Research on Learning* (where the book was written), and the company has incorporated the concept of the community of practice into its methods of management. As its applications to business received greater attention, the notion of the community of practice became a feature both of research in, and exercise of, knowledge management: the ways in which knowledge is produced, developed, shared, and put to use in an organization. The community of practice seemed to offer a social dimension for knowledge management relating to undocumented or unspoken knowledge.

The scholars John Seely Brown* and Paul Duguid,* for example, explored a classic case of informal social networking among Xerox photocopier technicians. These specialists often shared what they

> ❝ In general, situated learning focuses on some well-documented phenomena in cognitive psychology and ignores many others: while cognition is partly context-dependent, it is also partly context-independent; while there are dramatic failures of transfer, there are also dramatic successes; while concrete instruction helps, abstract instruction also helps; while some performances benefit from training in a social context, others do not. ❞
>
> John Anderson, Lynne Reder, and Herbert Simon, *Situated Learning and Education*

called "war stories" in the warehouse or over coffee, and sometimes received information for effective solutions that they would not have found in a manual.[1] The community-of-practice concept was also applied to the transmission of knowledge in other public organizations, such as in healthcare.

There was, however, criticism of the use of the community of practice as a tool of knowledge management: the idea was put to the service of managerial control over organizations, an idea Lave was not comfortable with. For his part, Wenger focused on trying to connect theory with reality.[2] Whichever interpretation one favors, it is a fact that conscious decisions have been taken to use the community of practice in organizations to achieve innovation and for the transmission of knowledge.

Interaction

The ideas of situated learning and the community of practice continue to be relevant; indeed, they are receiving increasing attention from both the academic world and from practitioners. The text still offers challenges to prevailing assumptions about knowledge and learning. Learning theory is greatly influenced by the book, and its contribution to the wider field of social theories of learning is undeniable.

Within organizational theory (theory relating to the nature and functioning of organizations), Lave and Wenger's *Situated Learning*, notably the idea of the community of practice, continues to offer a challenge to traditional management structures in organizations. New theories of organization must consider the question of how to accommodate the sometimes contradictory requirements of governance and development. The question remains: how to govern without governing, and how to teach without instructing?[3]

Among contemporary theories, activity theory* rivals in influence the theory of situated learning. Activity theory explores the role of factors such as the division of labor (the awarding of different tasks to different workers in order to achieve a particular end), the rules and tools useful to the learning process, and the wider structural characteristics that define learning in communities. Although activity theory is founded on the principle that practice serves a vital role in social systems, it differs considerably from the literature dealing with the community of practice as derived from the work of Lave and Wenger.

The Continuing Debate

For all *Situated Learning's* undoubted influence, there continue to be issues that provoke debate. For John Anderson* and Herbert Simon,* both psychologists* and computer scientists, and the psychologist Lynne Reder,* situated learning depends on certain claims not supported by practical research. With respect to the claim that "action is grounded in the situation in which it occurs,"[4] these authors note that some skills, such as reading, do in fact transfer from one context to another. The very fact that people can debate whether knowledge is dependent on context is, itself, evidence that reading and writing competences are *not* dependent on context.

Addressing the claim that "knowledge cannot be transferred between people independently of its context,"[5] they note that situated learning research has focused on cases where knowledge transfer has failed, and that there are cases where knowledge transfer has succeeded.

Regarding the claim that "teaching in abstract form has limited power,"[6] they argue that most modern information-processing theories involve "learning by doing," and argue that learning occurs best through a combination of abstract instruction with practice.

Finally, they respond to the claim that "complex environments are suitable for instruction"[7] with the argument that the best way forward for education is to combine methods that involve group work with methods that require tasks to be completed individually.

NOTES

1   John Seely Brown and Paul Duguid, "Organizational Learning and Communities-of-Practice: Toward a Unified View of Working, Learning, and Innovation," *Organization Science* 2, no.1 (1991): 40–57.

2   Etienne Wenger et al., *Cultivating Communities of Practice* (Boston: Harvard Business School Press, 2002).

3   Norman Makoto Su et al., "Doing Business with Theory: Communities of Practice in Knowledge Management," *Computer Supported Collaborative Work* 21, no. 2 (2012): 111–62.

4   John R. Anderson et al., "Situated Learning and Education," *Educational Researcher* 25, no. 4 (1996): 6.

5   Anderson et al., "Situated Learning," 6.

6   Anderson et al., "Situated Learning," 8.

7   Anderson et al., "Situated Learning," 9.

MODULE 12
WHERE NEXT?

KEY POINTS

- *Situated Learning* is likely to remain a highly relevant text; it may be considered a paradigm shift* (a dramatic change in common understanding) from theories of learning founded on cognition* to theories in which the social system where learning takes place is central.

- In the future, the text will probably have an impact on big debates about modern-day communities of practice,* including those that take place on social media, digital and virtual networks, and the Internet.

- *Situated Learning* remains one of the most relevant and cited works on theories of learning; it has been credited with stimulating the debate concerning the relevance of practice and psychological processes in the acquisition of knowledge.

Potential

Jean Lave and Etienne Wenger's *Situated Learning: Legitimate Peripheral Participation* will likely continue to be an influential text in the field of learning, even if we can expect some of its core ideas to continue to develop.

The text marks a fundamental shift from a cognitive approach to the understanding of learning toward approaches in which practice is central. Future ideas might look into how learning dynamics differ in various communities of practice. Are all practices equally powerful in the social world, or are there some with higher levels of power and some with lower? If these practices are different, what are the reasons for this? Are these differences rooted in the history of individual communities? Can we choose to empower specific practices to move

❝ You probably know that the earth is round and that
it is in orbit around the sun. But how do you know this?
What does it take? Obviously, it takes a brain in a living
body, but it also takes a very complex social, cultural
and historical system, which has accumulated learning
over time.**❞**

Etienne Wenger, *Communities of Practice and Social Learning Systems*

the social world in a particular direction, or does the empowerment
have to come from the participants themselves?

Similarly, future research might elaborate on the interactions
between agency* and learning that is conditional on place. This could
reveal why some individuals do better in certain communities of
practice than others.[1]

Moreover, with the development of social media, the Internet, and
other forms of digital communication, could there be new forms of
communities of practice? The emergence of these new forms, if they
are successfully adapted and accommodated, offers opportunities for
the development of the learning environment in social settings such as
educational institutions and organizations.

Future Directions

For champions of Lave and Wenger's ideas as set out in *Situated
Learning*, mind and body cannot be separated, and knowing and
practice are mutually constructed. To use academic terms, accepting
these statements entails a different ontological* perspective and
epistemological* stance ("ontology" being inquiry into the nature of
being; "epistemology" being inquiry into the nature of knowledge).
Practice theory considers the relationships between practice and
knowing, knowledge and knower, mind and body, and social and
individual. The arguments made by supporters must be evaluated

from this ontological and epistemological perspective, independent of the field of study or the setting for learning. Practice, activities, and objects of thought—knowledge—cannot be defined as independent entities.[2] They can only be defined in the light of the relations between them.

Summary

Revolutionizing theories of learning, *Situated Learning* is a pioneering text. It critically questions theories that, based on cognition, revolve around the psychological processes of individuals. It rejects the academic views on learning that form around the conventional separations of mind and body, knowledge and knower, teacher and learner. Instead, the book proposes an account of learning that prioritizes participation and access to practice—forms of activity—as the focus of learning. As such, the emphasis shifts from the individual to the relations between things in a social context.

Situated Learning is historically significant; when it was published in 1991, it addressed a genuine academic problem in learning studies regarding apprenticeship. Furthermore, the research outcomes were quickly adopted in the real world, led by the US technology corporation Xerox, the research sponsor, which applied the concept of the community of practice and found it beneficial to the way in which learning occurred within the company. The text will remain relevant for a long time because of the lack of rival theories to explain the role of the social system in learning. Inevitably, however, the book's theories will be adjusted and developed in ways that shift our understanding of the relationships between the individual, society, and learning.

NOTES

1   Lars Lindkvist, "Knowledge Communities and Knowledge Collectivities: A Typology of Knowledge Work in Groups," *Journal of Management Studies* 42, no. 6 (2005): 1189–210.

2   Jason Hughes et al., eds, *Communities of Practice: Critical Perspectives* (London: Routledge, 2007).

GLOSSARY

GLOSSARY OF TERMS

Activity theory: a theoretical approach to the interrelationships between activities and those performing the activities; these actors (individuals, organizations, or communities) are bound by an objective or a goal and are affected by the tools or instruments used to achieve the outcome.

Agency: the ability of an agent—a person capable of action—to act in the social world either in accordance with social structures, or in ways that challenge those structures.

Alcoholics Anonymous: an organization for alcoholics who seek to avoid alcohol and achieve sobriety by means of fellowship and shared practices.

Anthropology: the study of humanity in all its aspects, from evolution as species to social practices and cultural forms.

Apprenticeship: a form of training that involves following and studying a master of the trade on the job instead of in a school.

Artificial intelligence: intelligent behavior exhibited by computers.

Cognition/cognitive: mental processes of acquiring and understanding knowledge.

Cognitive learning theory: a theory founded on the assumption that learning is a process that takes place inside the mind.

Cognitive psychology: the study of the nature and functioning of cognition—thought, attention, language, the processing of knowledge, and so on—in the human mind.

Communities of practice (CoP): according to Wenger, these possess "a combination of three fundamental elements: a domain of knowledge, which defines a set of issues; a community of people who care about this domain; and the shared practice that they are developing to be effective in their domain."

CPsquare: an organization cofounded by Etienne Wenger that brings together teaching practitioners in order to share ideas about effective teaching techniques in order to help people learn.

Developmental studies: inquiry into the processes by which knowledge is acquired, and personality and identity are formed.

Empirical: founded on information that may be verified by observation.

Epistemology: the theory of knowledge—what distinguishes justified belief from mere opinion.

Figured worlds theory: a theory seeking to explain the ways in which identities are produced, particularly looking at the social types and culture that influence activities proposed by the social scientist Dorothy Holland.

Gola: a tribal people in the West African nation of Liberia.

Identity: the characteristics understood to determine who a person is and their place in society.

Institute for Research on Learning: a not-for-profit center of learning, now closed, founded by the Xerox Foundation (a philanthropic organization itself founded by the US technology corporation Xerox) and codirected by the computer scientist John Seely Brown at Palo Alto, California.

Internalization: an individual's acceptance of norms and values established by others.

Legitimate peripheral participation: a process through which newcomers become experienced members and eventually "old-timers" in a community of practice.

Linguistics: the study of language in terms of its form, its meaning, and context.

Old-timers: experienced and accepted members of a community of practice, who have been through the learning process.

Ontology: in analytical philosophy, the determination whether some categories of being are fundamental; ontology asks in what sense the items in those categories can be said to "be."

Paradigm shift: a termed coined by the US physicist, scientific philosopher, and scientific historian Thomas Kuhn (1922–96) to describe the nature of scientific revolutions.

Psychology: the study of the human mind and behavior.

Quartermaster: a military officer in charge of supplies and provisions.

Situated learning: learning that takes place in the same context in which it is applied.

Social anthropology: a division of anthropology concerned with the study of social structures and institutions and their interrelationships.

Social learning: a type of learning theory emphasizing the role of social context in learning, occurring through observation or direct instruction in the absence of other cognitive processes.

Social structure: ways of understanding a society in terms of the interaction between the different social groups ("working class," "upper class," "elite," and so on) that constitute it.

Vai: an ethnic group/language spoken in West Africa, predominantly in Liberia and Sierra Leone.

Yukatec Mayan: a language spoken in the Yucatan Peninsula and in northern Belize.

Zone of proximal development: the difference between what a learner can do without any instruction or help, and what he or she can do with instruction or help.

PEOPLE MENTIONED IN THE TEXT

John Anderson (b. 1947) is a professor of psychology and computer science at Carnegie Mellon University specializing in learning and computer based instruction.

Pierre Bourdieu (1930–2002) was a French sociologist, philosopher, and anthropologist. He was known particularly for his book *Distinction: A Social Critique of the Judgment of Taste* (1984) and more broadly for his research on power dynamics in society.

John Seely Brown (b. 1940) is an American researcher specializing in the impact of computer-supported activities on organizational learning.

Michael Cole (b. 1938) is a professor emeritus of communication and psychology at the University of California. His research focuses on cognitive development within cross-cultural contexts.

Alessia Contu is the chair in management and marketing at the University of Massachusetts, Boston. Her areas of research expertise include organization behavior, organization development, psychoanalysis, and ethical and social issues in management.

Sandra Dawson is professor emeritus of management studies at Judge Business School, University of Cambridge.

John Dewey (1859–1952) was an American psychologist, philosopher, educator, and social critic with influence in the field of social reform and education.

Paul Duguid is an adjunct professor at the University of California, Berkeley, specializing in the history of information. He was also a former member of the Institute for Research on Learning.

Yrjö Engeström is a professor of adult education and director of the Center for Research on Activity, Development and Learning (CRADLE) at the University of Helsinki in Finland. His work on activity theory and the zone of proximal development is relevant to situational learning.

Silvia Gherardi (b. 1949) is a professor of sociology of organization based at the University of Trento, Italy. Her research centers on workplace learning using qualitative methods.

Anthony Giddens (b. 1938) is a well-known British sociologist renowned for his work on the theory of structure and modern societies. His major publications include *New Rules of Sociological Method* (1976), *Central Problems in Social Theory* (1979), and *The Constitution of Society* (1984).

Christine Greenhow is an assistant professor in the college of education at Michigan State University, specializing in education and social media.

Jan Herrington is a professor of education at Murdoch University in Perth, Western Australia, doing research on authentic and mobile learning and design.

Dorothy Holland is a professor emeritus within change management (social, identity, agency, and social movements) at the University of North Carolina at Chapel Hill.

Jason Hughes is a professor of sociology at the University of Leicester, with research interests in the emotional aspects of management.

Brigitte Jordan is an influential anthropologist known for her work on tools and cross-cultural issues in obstetric and childbirth practices.

Bruce Kogut (b. 1953) is a professor of leadership and ethics based at the Columbia Business School. He is the director of the Sanford C. Bernstein Center for Leadership and Ethics.

Lars Lindkvist is professor of business administration at Linköping University in Sweden. His research focuses on creating methods and tools for simulation and evaluation of geometrical robustness.

Davide Nicolini is a professor and director of the Innovation, Knowledge & Organizational Networks Research Unit at Warwick Business School. His research deals with practice and change in organizations.

Eivor Oborn is a professor in healthcare management at Warwick Business School specializing in organizational theory and change, particularly within the subfields of collaboration and technology use within healthcare reforms.

Ron Oliver is a professor of teaching and administrator at Edith Cowan University, Western Australia.

Wanda Orlikowski is an information systems researcher and organizational theorist based at the Massachusetts Institute of Technology's Sloan School of Management. Her work involves studying the implementation and use of technologies within organizations.

Jean Piaget (1896–1980) was a Swiss psychologist regarded as the father of the study of cognitive development. He established the fields of cognitive theory and developmental psychology.

Lynne Reder is a professor specializing in learning and memory in Carnegie Mellon University's department of psychology.

Joanne Roberts is a professor in arts and cultural management at Winchester School of Art at the University of Southampton. Her research focuses on international business, creativity, and innovation.

Barbara Rogoff (b. 1950) is a distinguished professor of psychology at the University of California, Santa Cruz. Her research looks into cultural aspects of learning.

Sylvia Scribner (1923–91) was an American psychologist. Best-known for *The Psychology of Literacy* (1981), coauthored with Michael Cole, she focused on the role of culture in literacy and learning.

Herbert Simon (1916–2001) was a highly influential American social scientist renowned for his interdisciplinary approach. Among many other awards, he was the recipient of the Nobel Memorial Prize in Economics in 1978.

Lev Vygotsky (1896–1934) was a Russian psychologist known for his work within the fields of developmental psychology, child development, and education. He wrote several books including *Thought and Language* (1932).

Hugh Willmott is a professor in management and organization studies based at Cass Business School in London. He has published over 20 books and contributed to research in the development and application of management theory.

Udo Zander (b. 1959) is an assistant professor in international business based at the Stockholm School of Economics, specializing in international strategy and management research.

WORKS CITED

WORKS CITED

Anderson, John R., Lynne M. Reder, and Herbert A. Simon. "Situated Learning and Education." *Educational Researcher* 25, no. 4 (1996): 5–11.

Bourdieu, Pierre. *Outline of a Theory of Practice*. Translated by Richard Nice. Cambridge: Cambridge University Press, 1977.

Braun, Patrice. "Digital Knowledge Networks: Linking Communities of Practice with Innovation." *Journal of Business Strategies* 19, no. 1 (2002): 43.

Brown, John Seely, and Paul Duguid. "Organizational Learning and Communities-of-Practice: Toward a Unified View of Working, Learning, and Innovation." *Organization Science* 2, no.1 (1991): 40–57.

— — —. "Knowledge and Organization: A Social-Practice Perspective." *Organization Science* 12, no. 2 (2001): 198–213.

Contu, Alessia, and Hugh Willmott. "Re-Embedding Situatedness: The Importance of Power Relations in Learning Theory." *Organization Science* 14, no. 3 (2003): 283–96.

Cox, Andrew. "What Are Communities of Practice? A Comparative Review of Four Seminal Works." *Journal of Information Science* 31, no. 6 (2005): 527–40.

CPsquare. "Our Vision." Accessed January 20, 2016. http://cpsquare.org/vision/.

Dubé, Line, Anne Bourhis, and Réal Jacob. "The Impact of Structuring Characteristics on the Launching of Virtual Communities of Practice." *Journal of Organizational Change Management* 18, no. 2 (2005): 145–66.

Engeström, Yrjö. *Developmental Work Research: Expanding Activity Theory in Practice*. Berlin: Lehmanns Media, 2005.

Engeström, Yrjö, Reijo Miettinen, and Raija-Leena Punamäki. *Perspectives on Activity Theory*. Cambridge: Cambridge University Press, 1999.

Fox, Stephen. "Situated Learning Theory versus Traditional Cognitive Learning Theory: Why Management Education Should Not Ignore Management Learning." *Systemic Practice and Action Research* 10, no. 6 (1997): 727–47.

Gherardi, Silvia. "Practice-Based Theorizing on Learning and Knowing in Organizations." *Organization* 7, no. 2 (2000): 211–23.

Gherardi, Silvia, and Davide Nicolini. "To Transfer is to Transform: The Circulation of Safety Knowledge." *Organization* 7, no. 2 (2000): 329–48.

Giddens, Anthony. *The Constitution of Society: Outline of the Theory of Structuration*. Cambridge: Polity Press, 1984.

Greenhow, Christine, Beth Robelia, and Joan E. Hughes. "Learning, Teaching, and Scholarship in a Digital Age: Web 2.0 and Classroom Research—What Path Should We Take 'Now'?" *Educational Researcher* 38, no. 4 (2009): 246–59.

Herrington, Jan, and Ron Oliver. "Critical Characteristics of Situated Learning: Implications for the Instructional Design of Multimedia." murdoch.edu. au (1995). Accessed April 5, 2016. http://researchrepository.murdoch.edu. au/7189/1/critical_characteristics.pdf.

Hodkinson, Phil, and Heather Hodkinson. "A Constructive Critique of Communities of Practice: Moving Beyond Lave and Wenger." *OVAL Research Working Paper* (2004).

Holland, Dorothy. *Identity and Agency in Cultural Worlds*. Cambridge, MA: Harvard University Press, 2001.

Holland, Dorothy, and Jean Lave. "Social Practice Theory and the Historical Production of Persons." *Actio: An International Journal of Human Activity Theory* 2 (2009): 1–15.

Hughes, Jason, Nick Jewson, and Lorna Unwin, eds. *Communities of Practice: Critical Perspectives*. London: Routledge, 2007.

Infed.org. "Jean Lave, Etienne Wenger and Communities of Practice." Accessed November 20, 2015. http://infed.org/mobi/jean-lave-etienne-wenger-and-communities-of-practice.

Jordan, Brigitte. "Cosmopolitical Obstetrics: Some Insights from the Training of Traditional Midwives." *Social Science & Medicine* 28, no. 9 (1989): 925–37.

Kogut, Bruce, and Udo Zander. "What Firms Do? Coordination, Identity, and Learning." *Organization Science* 7, no. 5 (1996): 502–18.

Lave, Jean. *Cognition in Practice: Mind, Mathematics and Culture in Everyday Life*. Cambridge: Cambridge University Press, 1988.

Lave, Jean, and Etienne Wenger. *Situated Learning: Legitimate Peripheral Participation*. Cambridge: Cambridge University Press, 1991.

Lervik, Jon Erland, Kathryn M. Fahy, and Mark Easterby-Smith. "Temporal Dynamics of Situated Learning in Organizations." *Management Learning* 41, no. 3 (2010): 285–301.

Lindkvist, Lars. "Knowledge Communities and Knowledge Collectivities: A Typology of Knowledge Work in Groups." *Journal of Management Studies* 42, no. 6 (2005): 1189–210.

Murillo, Enrique. "Communities of Practice in the Business and Organization Studies Literature." *Information Research* 16, no. 1 (2011): 1.

Oborn, Eivor, and Sandra Dawson. "Learning across Communities of Practice: An Examination of Multidisciplinary Work." *British Journal of Management* 21, no. 4 (2010): 843–58.

Orlikowski, Wanda J. "Knowing in Practice: Enacting a Collective Capability in Distributed Organizing." *Organization Science* 13, no. 3 (2002): 249–73.

Piaget, Jean. *The Origins of Intelligence in Children*. New York: International University Press, 1952.

Roberts, Joanne. "Limits to Communities of Practice." *Journal of Management Studies* 43, no. 3 (2006): 623–39.

Rogoff, Barbara, and Jean Lave, eds. *Everyday Cognition: Its Development in Social Context*. Cambridge, MA: Harvard University Press, 1984.

Scribner, Silvia, and Michael Cole. *The Psychology of Literacy*. Cambridge, MA: Harvard University Press, 1981.

Sfard, Anna, and Anna Prusak. "Telling Identities: In Search of an Analytic Tool for Investigating Learning as a Culturally Shaped Activity." *Educational Researcher* 34, no. 4 (2005): 14–22.

Su, Norman Makoto, Hiroko N. Wilensky, and David F. Redmiles. "Doing Business with Theory: Communities of Practice in Knowledge Management." *Computer Supported Collaborative Work* 21, no. 2 (2012): 111–62.

Vygotsky, Lev Semyonovich. *Educational Psychology*. Cambridge, MA: MIT, 1926.

— — —. *Mind in Society: The Development of Higher Psychological Processes*. Cambridge, MA: Harvard University Press, 1980.

Wenger, Etienne. *Communities of Practice: Learning, Meaning, and Identity*. Cambridge: Cambridge University Press, 1998.

— — —. "Communities of Practice and Social Learning Systems: The Career of a Concept." In *Social Learning Systems and Communities of Practice*, edited by Chris Blackmore, 179–98. London: Springer, 2010.

Wenger, Etienne, Richard McDermott, and William M. Snyder. *Cultivating Communities of Practice: A Guide to Managing Knowledge*. Boston: Harvard Business School Press, 2002.

Wenger, Etienne, Nancy White, and John D. Smith. *Digital Habitats*. Portland, OR: CPsquare, 2009.

THE MACAT LIBRARY
BY DISCIPLINE

AFRICANA STUDIES

Chinua Achebe's *An Image of Africa: Racism in Conrad's Heart of Darkness*
W. E. B. Du Bois's *The Souls of Black Folk*
Zora Neale Huston's *Characteristics of Negro Expression*
Martin Luther King Jr's *Why We Can't Wait*
Toni Morrison's *Playing in the Dark: Whiteness in the American Literary Imagination*

ANTHROPOLOGY

Arjun Appadurai's *Modernity at Large: Cultural Dimensions of Globalisation*
Philippe Ariès's *Centuries of Childhood*
Franz Boas's *Race, Language and Culture*
Kim Chan & Renée Mauborgne's *Blue Ocean Strategy*
Jared Diamond's *Guns, Germs & Steel: the Fate of Human Societies*
Jared Diamond's *Collapse: How Societies Choose to Fail or Survive*
E. E. Evans-Pritchard's *Witchcraft, Oracles and Magic Among the Azande*
James Ferguson's *The Anti-Politics Machine*
Clifford Geertz's *The Interpretation of Cultures*
David Graeber's *Debt: the First 5000 Years*
Karen Ho's *Liquidated: An Ethnography of Wall Street*
Geert Hofstede's *Culture's Consequences: Comparing Values, Behaviors, Institutes and Organizations across Nations*
Claude Lévi-Strauss's *Structural Anthropology*
Jay Macleod's *Ain't No Makin' It: Aspirations and Attainment in a Low-Income Neighborhood*
Saba Mahmood's *The Politics of Piety: The Islamic Revival and the Feminist Subjec*t
Marcel Mauss's *The Gift*

BUSINESS

Jean Lave & Etienne Wenger's *Situated Learning*
Theodore Levitt's *Marketing Myopia*
Burton G. Malkiel's *A Random Walk Down Wall Street*
Douglas McGregor's *The Human Side of Enterprise*
Michael Porter's *Competitive Strategy: Creating and Sustaining Superior Performance*
John Kotter's *Leading Change*
C. K. Prahalad & Gary Hamel's *The Core Competence of the Corporation*

CRIMINOLOGY

Michelle Alexander's *The New Jim Crow: Mass Incarceration in the Age of Colorblindness*
Michael R. Gottfredson & Travis Hirschi's *A General Theory of Crime*
Richard Herrnstein & Charles A. Murray's *The Bell Curve: Intelligence and Class Structure in American Life*
Elizabeth Loftus's *Eyewitness Testimony*
Jay Macleod's *Ain't No Makin' It: Aspirations and Attainment in a Low-Income Neighborhood*
Philip Zimbardo's *The Lucifer Effect*

ECONOMICS

Janet Abu-Lughod's *Before European Hegemony*
Ha-Joon Chang's *Kicking Away the Ladder*
David Brion Davis's *The Problem of Slavery in the Age of Revolution*
Milton Friedman's *The Role of Monetary Policy*
Milton Friedman's *Capitalism and Freedom*
David Graeber's *Debt: the First 5000 Years*
Friedrich Hayek's *The Road to Serfdom*
Karen Ho's *Liquidated: An Ethnography of Wall Street*

John Maynard Keynes's *The General Theory of Employment, Interest and Money*
Charles P. Kindleberger's *Manias, Panics and Crashes*
Robert Lucas's *Why Doesn't Capital Flow from Rich to Poor Countries?*
Burton G. Malkiel's *A Random Walk Down Wall Street*
Thomas Robert Malthus's *An Essay on the Principle of Population*
Karl Marx's *Capital*
Thomas Piketty's *Capital in the Twenty-First Century*
Amartya Sen's *Development as Freedom*
Adam Smith's *The Wealth of Nations*
Nassim Nicholas Taleb's *The Black Swan: The Impact of the Highly Improbable*
Amos Tversky's & Daniel Kahneman's *Judgment under Uncertainty: Heuristics and Biases*
Mahbub Ul Haq's *Reflections on Human Development*
Max Weber's *The Protestant Ethic and the Spirit of Capitalism*

FEMINISM AND GENDER STUDIES

Judith Butler's *Gender Trouble*
Simone De Beauvoir's *The Second Sex*
Michel Foucault's *History of Sexuality*
Betty Friedan's *The Feminine Mystique*
Saba Mahmood's *The Politics of Piety: The Islamic Revival and the Feminist Subject*
Joan Wallach Scott's *Gender and the Politics of History*
Mary Wollstonecraft's *A Vindication of the Rights of Woman*
Virginia Woolf's *A Room of One's Own*

GEOGRAPHY

The Brundtland Report's *Our Common Future*
Rachel Carson's *Silent Spring*
Charles Darwin's *On the Origin of Species*
James Ferguson's *The Anti-Politics Machine*
Jane Jacobs's *The Death and Life of Great American Cities*
James Lovelock's *Gaia: A New Look at Life on Earth*
Amartya Sen's *Development as Freedom*
Mathis Wackernagel & William Rees's *Our Ecological Footprint*

HISTORY

Janet Abu-Lughod's *Before European Hegemony*
Benedict Anderson's *Imagined Communities*
Bernard Bailyn's *The Ideological Origins of the American Revolution*
Hanna Batatu's *The Old Social Classes And The Revolutionary Movements Of Iraq*
Christopher Browning's *Ordinary Men: Reserve Police Batallion 101 and the Final Solution in Poland*
Edmund Burke's *Reflections on the Revolution in France*
William Cronon's *Nature's Metropolis: Chicago And The Great West*
Alfred W. Crosby's *The Columbian Exchange*
Hamid Dabashi's *Iran: A People Interrupted*
David Brion Davis's *The Problem of Slavery in the Age of Revolution*
Nathalie Zemon Davis's *The Return of Martin Guerre*
Jared Diamond's *Guns, Germs & Steel: the Fate of Human Societies*
Frank Dikotter's *Mao's Great Famine*
John W Dower's *War Without Mercy: Race And Power In The Pacific War*
W. E. B. Du Bois's *The Souls of Black Folk*
Richard J. Evans's *In Defence of History*
Lucien Febvre's *The Problem of Unbelief in the 16th Century*
Sheila Fitzpatrick's *Everyday Stalinism*

Eric Foner's *Reconstruction: America's Unfinished Revolution, 1863-1877*
Michel Foucault's *Discipline and Punish*
Michel Foucault's *History of Sexuality*
Francis Fukuyama's *The End of History and the Last Man*
John Lewis Gaddis's *We Now Know: Rethinking Cold War History*
Ernest Gellner's *Nations and Nationalism*
Eugene Genovese's *Roll, Jordan, Roll: The World the Slaves Made*
Carlo Ginzburg's *The Night Battles*
Daniel Goldhagen's *Hitler's Willing Executioners*
Jack Goldstone's *Revolution and Rebellion in the Early Modern World*
Antonio Gramsci's *The Prison Notebooks*
Alexander Hamilton, John Jay & James Madison's *The Federalist Papers*
Christopher Hill's *The World Turned Upside Down*
Carole Hillenbrand's *The Crusades: Islamic Perspectives*
Thomas Hobbes's *Leviathan*
Eric Hobsbawm's *The Age Of Revolution*
John A. Hobson's *Imperialism: A Study*
Albert Hourani's *History of the Arab Peoples*
Samuel P. Huntington's *The Clash of Civilizations and the Remaking of World Order*
C. L. R. James's *The Black Jacobins*
Tony Judt's *Postwar: A History of Europe Since 1945*
Ernst Kantorowicz's *The King's Two Bodies: A Study in Medieval Political Theology*
Paul Kennedy's *The Rise and Fall of the Great Powers*
Ian Kershaw's *The "Hitler Myth": Image and Reality in the Third Reich*
John Maynard Keynes's *The General Theory of Employment, Interest and Money*
Charles P. Kindleberger's *Manias, Panics and Crashes*
Martin Luther King Jr's *Why We Can't Wait*
Henry Kissinger's *World Order: Reflections on the Character of Nations and the Course of History*
Thomas Kuhn's *The Structure of Scientific Revolutions*
Georges Lefebvre's *The Coming of the French Revolution*
John Locke's *Two Treatises of Government*
Niccolò Machiavelli's *The Prince*
Thomas Robert Malthus's *An Essay on the Principle of Population*
Mahmood Mamdani's *Citizen and Subject: Contemporary Africa And The Legacy Of Late Colonialism*
Karl Marx's *Capital*
Stanley Milgram's *Obedience to Authority*
John Stuart Mill's *On Liberty*
Thomas Paine's *Common Sense*
Thomas Paine's *Rights of Man*
Geoffrey Parker's *Global Crisis: War, Climate Change and Catastrophe in the Seventeenth Century*
Jonathan Riley-Smith's *The First Crusade and the Idea of Crusading*
Jean-Jacques Rousseau's *The Social Contract*
Joan Wallach Scott's *Gender and the Politics of History*
Theda Skocpol's *States and Social Revolutions*
Adam Smith's *The Wealth of Nations*
Timothy Snyder's *Bloodlands: Europe Between Hitler and Stalin*
Sun Tzu's *The Art of War*
Keith Thomas's *Religion and the Decline of Magic*
Thucydides's *The History of the Peloponnesian War*
Frederick Jackson Turner's *The Significance of the Frontier in American History*
Odd Arne Westad's *The Global Cold War: Third World Interventions And The Making Of Our Times*

LITERATURE

Chinua Achebe's *An Image of Africa: Racism in Conrad's Heart of Darkness*
Roland Barthes's *Mythologies*
Homi K. Bhabha's *The Location of Culture*
Judith Butler's *Gender Trouble*
Simone De Beauvoir's *The Second Sex*
Ferdinand De Saussure's *Course in General Linguistics*
T. S. Eliot's *The Sacred Wood: Essays on Poetry and Criticism*
Zora Neale Huston's *Characteristics of Negro Expression*
Toni Morrison's *Playing in the Dark: Whiteness in the American Literary Imagination*
Edward Said's *Orientalism*
Gayatri Chakravorty Spivak's *Can the Subaltern Speak?*
Mary Wollstonecraft's *A Vindication of the Rights of Women*
Virginia Woolf's *A Room of One's Own*

PHILOSOPHY

Elizabeth Anscombe's *Modern Moral Philosophy*
Hannah Arendt's *The Human Condition*
Aristotle's *Metaphysics*
Aristotle's *Nicomachean Ethics*
Edmund Gettier's *Is Justified True Belief Knowledge?*
Georg Wilhelm Friedrich Hegel's *Phenomenology of Spirit*
David Hume's *Dialogues Concerning Natural Religion*
David Hume's *The Enquiry for Human Understanding*
Immanuel Kant's *Religion within the Boundaries of Mere Reason*
Immanuel Kant's *Critique of Pure Reason*
Søren Kierkegaard's *The Sickness Unto Death*
Søren Kierkegaard's *Fear and Trembling*
C. S. Lewis's *The Abolition of Man*
Alasdair MacIntyre's *After Virtue*
Marcus Aurelius's *Meditations*
Friedrich Nietzsche's *On the Genealogy of Morality*
Friedrich Nietzsche's *Beyond Good and Evil*
Plato's *Republic*
Plato's *Symposium*
Jean-Jacques Rousseau's *The Social Contract*
Gilbert Ryle's *The Concept of Mind*
Baruch Spinoza's *Ethics*
Sun Tzu's *The Art of War*
Ludwig Wittgenstein's *Philosophical Investigations*

POLITICS

Benedict Anderson's *Imagined Communities*
Aristotle's *Politics*
Bernard Bailyn's *The Ideological Origins of the American Revolution*
Edmund Burke's *Reflections on the Revolution in France*
John C. Calhoun's *A Disquisition on Government*
Ha-Joon Chang's *Kicking Away the Ladder*
Hamid Dabashi's *Iran: A People Interrupted*
Hamid Dabashi's *Theology of Discontent: The Ideological Foundation of the Islamic Revolution in Iran*
Robert Dahl's *Democracy and its Critics*
Robert Dahl's *Who Governs?*
David Brion Davis's *The Problem of Slavery in the Age of Revolution*

Alexis De Tocqueville's *Democracy in America*
James Ferguson's *The Anti-Politics Machine*
Frank Dikotter's *Mao's Great Famine*
Sheila Fitzpatrick's *Everyday Stalinism*
Eric Foner's *Reconstruction: America's Unfinished Revolution, 1863-1877*
Milton Friedman's *Capitalism and Freedom*
Francis Fukuyama's *The End of History and the Last Man*
John Lewis Gaddis's *We Now Know: Rethinking Cold War History*
Ernest Gellner's *Nations and Nationalism*
David Graeber's *Debt: the First 5000 Years*
Antonio Gramsci's *The Prison Notebooks*
Alexander Hamilton, John Jay & James Madison's *The Federalist Papers*
Friedrich Hayek's *The Road to Serfdom*
Christopher Hill's *The World Turned Upside Down*
Thomas Hobbes's *Leviathan*
John A. Hobson's *Imperialism: A Study*
Samuel P. Huntington's *The Clash of Civilizations and the Remaking of World Order*
Tony Judt's *Postwar: A History of Europe Since 1945*
David C. Kang's *China Rising: Peace, Power and Order in East Asia*
Paul Kennedy's *The Rise and Fall of Great Powers*
Robert Keohane's *After Hegemony*
Martin Luther King Jr.'s *Why We Can't Wait*
Henry Kissinger's *World Order: Reflections on the Character of Nations and the Course of History*
John Locke's *Two Treatises of Government*
Niccolò Machiavelli's *The Prince*
Thomas Robert Malthus's *An Essay on the Principle of Population*
Mahmood Mamdani's *Citizen and Subject: Contemporary Africa And The Legacy Of Late Colonialism*
Karl Marx's *Capital*
John Stuart Mill's *On Liberty*
John Stuart Mill's *Utilitarianism*
Hans Morgenthau's *Politics Among Nations*
Thomas Paine's *Common Sense*
Thomas Paine's *Rights of Man*
Thomas Piketty's *Capital in the Twenty-First Century*
Robert D. Putman's *Bowling Alone*
John Rawls's *Theory of Justice*
Jean-Jacques Rousseau's *The Social Contract*
Theda Skocpol's *States and Social Revolutions*
Adam Smith's *The Wealth of Nations*
Sun Tzu's *The Art of War*
Henry David Thoreau's *Civil Disobedience*
Thucydides's *The History of the Peloponnesian War*
Kenneth Waltz's *Theory of International Politics*
Max Weber's *Politics as a Vocation*
Odd Arne Westad's *The Global Cold War: Third World Interventions And The Making Of Our Times*

POSTCOLONIAL STUDIES

Roland Barthes's *Mythologies*
Frantz Fanon's *Black Skin, White Masks*
Homi K. Bhabha's *The Location of Culture*
Gustavo Gutiérrez's *A Theology of Liberation*
Edward Said's *Orientalism*
Gayatri Chakravorty Spivak's *Can the Subaltern Speak?*

PSYCHOLOGY

Gordon Allport's *The Nature of Prejudice*
Alan Baddeley & Graham Hitch's *Aggression: A Social Learning Analysis*
Albert Bandura's *Aggression: A Social Learning Analysis*
Leon Festinger's *A Theory of Cognitive Dissonance*
Sigmund Freud's *The Interpretation of Dreams*
Betty Friedan's *The Feminine Mystique*
Michael R. Gottfredson & Travis Hirschi's *A General Theory of Crime*
Eric Hoffer's *The True Believer: Thoughts on the Nature of Mass Movements*
William James's *Principles of Psychology*
Elizabeth Loftus's *Eyewitness Testimony*
A. H. Maslow's *A Theory of Human Motivation*
Stanley Milgram's *Obedience to Authority*
Steven Pinker's *The Better Angels of Our Nature*
Oliver Sacks's *The Man Who Mistook His Wife For a Hat*
Richard Thaler & Cass Sunstein's *Nudge: Improving Decisions About Health, Wealth and Happiness*
Amos Tversky's *Judgment under Uncertainty: Heuristics and Biases*
Philip Zimbardo's *The Lucifer Effect*

SCIENCE

Rachel Carson's *Silent Spring*
William Cronon's *Nature's Metropolis: Chicago And The Great West*
Alfred W. Crosby's *The Columbian Exchange*
Charles Darwin's *On the Origin of Species*
Richard Dawkin's *The Selfish Gene*
Thomas Kuhn's *The Structure of Scientific Revolutions*
Geoffrey Parker's *Global Crisis: War, Climate Change and Catastrophe in the Seventeenth Century*
Mathis Wackernagel & William Rees's *Our Ecological Footprint*

SOCIOLOGY

Michelle Alexander's *The New Jim Crow: Mass Incarceration in the Age of Colorblindness*
Gordon Allport's *The Nature of Prejudice*
Albert Bandura's *Aggression: A Social Learning Analysis*
Hanna Batatu's *The Old Social Classes And The Revolutionary Movements Of Iraq*
Ha-Joon Chang's *Kicking Away the Ladder*
W. E. B. Du Bois's *The Souls of Black Folk*
Émile Durkheim's *On Suicide*
Frantz Fanon's *Black Skin, White Masks*
Frantz Fanon's *The Wretched of the Earth*
Eric Foner's *Reconstruction: America's Unfinished Revolution, 1863-1877*
Eugene Genovese's *Roll, Jordan, Roll: The World the Slaves Made*
Jack Goldstone's *Revolution and Rebellion in the Early Modern World*
Antonio Gramsci's *The Prison Notebooks*
Richard Herrnstein & Charles A Murray's *The Bell Curve: Intelligence and Class Structure in American Life*
Eric Hoffer's *The True Believer: Thoughts on the Nature of Mass Movements*
Jane Jacobs's *The Death and Life of Great American Cities*
Robert Lucas's *Why Doesn't Capital Flow from Rich to Poor Countries?*
Jay Macleod's *Ain't No Makin' It: Aspirations and Attainment in a Low Income Neighborhood*
Elaine May's *Homeward Bound: American Families in the Cold War Era*
Douglas McGregor's *The Human Side of Enterprise*
C. Wright Mills's *The Sociological Imagination*

Thomas Piketty's *Capital in the Twenty-First Century*
Robert D. Putman's *Bowling Alone*
David Riesman's *The Lonely Crowd: A Study of the Changing American Character*
Edward Said's *Orientalism*
Joan Wallach Scott's *Gender and the Politics of History*
Theda Skocpol's *States and Social Revolutions*
Max Weber's *The Protestant Ethic and the Spirit of Capitalism*

THEOLOGY

Augustine's *Confessions*
Benedict's *Rule of St Benedict*
Gustavo Gutiérrez's *A Theology of Liberation*
Carole Hillenbrand's *The Crusades: Islamic Perspectives*
David Hume's *Dialogues Concerning Natural Religion*
Immanuel Kant's *Religion within the Boundaries of Mere Reason*
Ernst Kantorowicz's *The King's Two Bodies: A Study in Medieval Political Theology*
Søren Kierkegaard's *The Sickness Unto Death*
C. S. Lewis's *The Abolition of Man*
Saba Mahmood's *The Politics of Piety: The Islamic Revival and the Feminist Subjec*t
Baruch Spinoza's *Ethics*
Keith Thomas's *Religion and the Decline of Magic*

COMING SOON

Chris Argyris's *The Individual and the Organisation*
Seyla Benhabib's *The Rights of Others*
Walter Benjamin's *The Work Of Art in the Age of Mechanical Reproduction*
John Berger's *Ways of Seeing*
Pierre Bourdieu's *Outline of a Theory of Practice*
Mary Douglas's *Purity and Danger*
Roland Dworkin's *Taking Rights Seriously*
James G. March's *Exploration and Exploitation in Organisational Learning*
Ikujiro Nonaka's *A Dynamic Theory of Organizational Knowledge Creation*
Griselda Pollock's *Vision and Difference*
Amartya Sen's *Inequality Re-Examined*
Susan Sontag's *On Photography*
Yasser Tabbaa's *The Transformation of Islamic Art*
Ludwig von Mises's *Theory of Money and Credit*

Macat Disciplines

Access the greatest ideas and thinkers across entire disciplines, including

Postcolonial Studies

Roland Barthes's *Mythologies*
Frantz Fanon's *Black Skin, White Masks*
Homi K. Bhabha's *The Location of Culture*
Gustavo Gutiérrez's *A Theology of Liberation*
Edward Said's *Orientalism*
Gayatri Chakravorty Spivak's *Can the Subaltern Speak?*

Macat analyses are available from all good bookshops and libraries.

Access hundreds of analyses through one, multimedia tool.
Join free for one month **library.macat.com**

Macat Disciplines

Access the greatest ideas and thinkers across entire disciplines, including

AFRICANA STUDIES

Chinua Achebe's *An Image of Africa: Racism in Conrad's Heart of Darkness*

W. E. B. Du Bois's *The Souls of Black Folk*

Zora Neale Hurston's *Characteristics of Negro Expression*

Martin Luther King Jr.'s *Why We Can't Wait*

Toni Morrison's *Playing in the Dark: Whiteness in the American Literary Imagination*

Macat analyses are available from all good bookshops and libraries.

Access hundreds of analyses through one, multimedia tool.
Join free for one month **library.macat.com**

Macat Disciplines

Access the greatest ideas and thinkers across entire disciplines, including

FEMINISM, GENDER AND QUEER STUDIES

Simone De Beauvoir's
The Second Sex

Michel Foucault's
History of Sexuality

Betty Friedan's
The Feminine Mystique

Saba Mahmood's
*The Politics of Piety:
The Islamic Revival and
the Feminist Subject*

Joan Wallach Scott's
*Gender and the
Politics of History*

Mary Wollstonecraft's
*A Vindication of the
Rights of Woman*

Virginia Woolf's
A Room of One's Own

Judith Butler's
Gender Trouble

Macat analyses are available from all good bookshops and libraries.

Access hundreds of analyses through one, multimedia tool.
Join free for one month **library.macat.com**

Macat Disciplines

Access the greatest ideas and thinkers across entire disciplines, including

CRIMINOLOGY

Michelle Alexander's
The New Jim Crow:
Mass Incarceration in the
Age of Colorblindness

Michael R. Gottfredson
& Travis Hirschi's
A General Theory of Crime

Elizabeth Loftus's
Eyewitness Testimony

Richard Herrnstein
& Charles A. Murray's
The Bell Curve: Intelligence and
Class Structure in American Life

Jay Macleod's
Ain't No Makin' It:
Aspirations and Attainment in a
Low-Income Neighborhood

Philip Zimbardo's
The Lucifer Effect

Macat analyses are available from all good bookshops and libraries.

Access hundreds of analyses through one, multimedia tool.
Join free for one month **library.macat.com**

Macat Disciplines

Access the greatest ideas and thinkers across entire disciplines, including

INEQUALITY

Ha-Joon Chang's, *Kicking Away the Ladder*

David Graeber's, *Debt: The First 5000 Years*

Robert E. Lucas's, *Why Doesn't Capital Flow from Rich To Poor Countries?*

Thomas Piketty's, *Capital in the Twenty-First Century*

Amartya Sen's, *Inequality Re-Examined*

Mahbub Ul Haq's, *Reflections on Human Development*

Macat analyses are available from all good bookshops and libraries.

Access hundreds of analyses through one, multimedia tool.
Join free for one month **library.macat.com**

Macat Disciplines

Access the greatest ideas and thinkers across entire disciplines, including

GLOBALIZATION

Arjun Appadurai's, *Modernity at Large: Cultural Dimensions of Globalisation*

James Ferguson's, *The Anti-Politics Machine*

Geert Hofstede's, *Culture's Consequences*

Amartya Sen's, *Development as Freedom*

Macat analyses are available from all good bookshops and libraries.

Access hundreds of analyses through one, multimedia tool.
Join free for one month **library.macat.com**

Macat Disciplines

Access the greatest ideas and thinkers across entire disciplines, including

MAN AND THE ENVIRONMENT

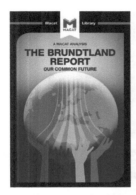

The Brundtland Report's, *Our Common Future*

Rachel Carson's, *Silent Spring*

James Lovelock's, *Gaia: A New Look at Life on Earth*

Mathis Wackernagel & William Rees's, *Our Ecological Footprint*

Macat analyses are available from all good bookshops and libraries.

Access hundreds of analyses through one, multimedia tool.
Join free for one month **library.macat.com**

Macat Disciplines

Access the greatest ideas and thinkers across entire disciplines, including

THE FUTURE OF DEMOCRACY

Robert A. Dahl's, *Democracy and Its Critics*
Robert A. Dahl's, *Who Governs?*
Alexis De Toqueville's, *Democracy in America*
Niccolò Machiavelli's, *The Prince*
John Stuart Mill's, *On Liberty*
Robert D. Putnam's, *Bowling Alone*
Jean-Jacques Rousseau's, *The Social Contract*
Henry David Thoreau's, *Civil Disobedience*

Macat analyses are available from all good bookshops and libraries.

Access hundreds of analyses through one, multimedia tool.
Join free for one month **library.macat.com**

Macat Disciplines

Access the greatest ideas and thinkers across entire disciplines, including

TOTALITARIANISM

Sheila Fitzpatrick's, *Everyday Stalinism*
Ian Kershaw's, *The "Hitler Myth"*
Timothy Snyder's, *Bloodlands*